Large-Paper Edition

THE COMPLETE POETICAL WORKS

OF

WILLIAM WORDSWORTH

IN TEN VOLUMES

VOLUME IX

William Wordsworth
From the painting by Haydon, 1842

THE
COMPLETE POETICAL WORKS

OF

William Wordsworth

IX

LAST POEMS

BOSTON AND NEW YORK

HOUGHTON MIFFLIN COMPANY

MDCCCCXI

CONTENTS

[v]

CONTENTS

CONTENTS

CONTENTS

CONTENTS

[ix]

CONTENTS

[x]

CONTENTS

[xi]

CONTENTS

[xii]

CONTENTS

CONTENTS

CONTENTS

[xv]

CONTENTS

NOTES ON THE ILLUSTRATIONS

From a painting by Benjamin Robert Haydon, 1842. The artist represented Wordsworth in this picture as if ascending Helvellyn and composing the sonnet addressed to himself (Haydon) on his portrait of the Duke of Wellington upon the field of Waterloo. This sonnet was written in 1840. The portrait represents Wordsworth in his seventy-second year. A copy sent by the artist to Miss E. B. Barrett (afterwards Mrs. Browning) inspired her to write the following sonnet: —

"Wordsworth upon Helvellyn! Let the cloud
  Ebb audibly along the mountain-wind,
  Then break against the rock, and show behind
  The lowland valleys floating up to crowd
  The sense with beauty. He with forehead bowed
And humble-lidded eyes, as one inclined
Before the sovran thought of his own mind,
And very meek with inspirations proud,
Takes here his rightful place as poet-priest
By the high altar, singing prayer and prayer
To the higher Heavens. A noble vision free
Our Haydon's hand has flung out from the mist!
No portrait this, with Academic air !
This is the poet and his poetry."

NOTES ON THE ILLUSTRATIONS

"What though our burthen be not light,
We need not toil from morn to night."

"Life with yon Lambs, like day, is just begun."

"The most alluring clouds that mount the sky
Owe to a troubled element their forms,
Their hues to sunset."

"His flock, along the woodland's edge with relics
sprinkled o'er
Of last night's snow, beneath a sky threatening the
fall of more,
Where tufts of herbage tempted each, were busy at
their feed."

"The brook itself,
Old as the hills that feed it from afar,
Doth rather deepen than disturb the calm."

"Behold an emblem of our human mind
Crowded with thoughts that need a settled home,
Yet, like to eddying balls of foam
Within this whirlpool, they each other chase
Round and round, and neither find
An outlet nor a resting-place!"

POEMS
1834–1847

POEMS
1843–1847

"NOT IN THE LUCID INTERVALS OF LIFE"

1834   1835

The lines following "nor do words" were written with Lord Byron's character, as a poet, before me, and that of others, his contemporaries, who wrote under like influences.

Not in the lucid intervals of life
That come but as a curse to party-strife;
Not in some hour when Pleasure with a sigh
Of languor puts his rosy garland by;
Not in the breathing-times of that poor slave
Who daily piles up wealth in Mammon's cave —
Is Nature felt, or can be; nor do words,
Which practised talent readily affords,
Prove that her hand has touched responsive chords;
Nor has her gentle beauty power to move
With genuine rapture and with fervent love
The soul of Genius, if he dare to take
Life's rule from passion craved for passion's sake;
Untaught that meekness is the cherished bent

[3]

NOT IN THE LUCID INTERVALS OF LIFE

Of all the truly great and all the innocent.
   But who is innocent? By grace divine,
Not otherwise, O Nature! we are thine,
Through good and evil thine, in just degree
Of rational and manly sympathy.
To all that Earth from pensive hearts is stealing,
And Heaven is now to gladdened eyes revealing,
Add every charm the Universe can show
Through every change its aspects undergo —
Care may be respited, but not repealed;
No perfect cure grows on that bounded field.
Vain is the pleasure, a false calm the peace,
If He, through whom alone our conflicts cease,
Our virtuous hopes without relapse advance,
Come not to speed the Soul's deliverance;
To the distempered Intellect refuse
His gracious help, or give what we abuse.

BY THE SIDE OF RYDAL MERE

1834   1835

THE linnet's warble, sinking towards a close,
Hints to the thrush 't is time for their repose;
The shrill-voiced thrush is heedless, and again
The monitor revives his own sweet strain;
But both will soon be mastered, and the copse
Be left as silent as the mountain-tops,
Ere some commanding star dismiss to rest
The throng of rooks, that now, from twig or nest,
(After a steady flight on home-bound wings,
And a last game of mazy hoverings
Around their ancient grove) with cawing noise
Disturb the liquid music's equipoise.

O Nightingale! Who ever heard thy song
Might here be moved, till Fancy grows so strong
That listening sense is pardonably cheated
Where wood or stream by thee was never greeted.
Surely, from fairest spots of favoured lands,
Were not some gifts withheld by jealous hands,
This hour of deepening darkness here would be
As a fresh morning for new harmony;
And lays as prompt would hail the dawn of Night:

BY THE SIDE OF RYDAL MERE

A *dawn* she has both beautiful and bright,
When the East kindles with the full moon's light;
Not like the rising sun's impatient glow
Dazzling the mountains, but an overflow
Of solemn splendour, in mutation slow.

   Wanderer by spring with gradual progress led,
For sway profoundly felt as widely spread;
To king, to peasant, to rough sailor, dear,
And to the soldier's trumpet-wearied ear;
How welcome wouldst thou be to this green Vale
Fairer than Tempe! Yet, sweet Nightingale!
From the warm breeze that bears thee on, alight
At will, and stay thy migratory flight;
Build, at thy choice, or sing, by pool or fount,
Who shall complain, or call thee to account?
The wisest, happiest, of our kind are they
That ever walk content with Nature's way,
God's goodness — measuring bounty as it may;
For whom the gravest thought of what they miss,
Chastening the fulness of a present bliss,
Is with that wholesome office satisfied,
While unrepining sadness is allied
In thankful bosoms to a modest pride.

"SOFT AS A CLOUD IS YON BLUE RIDGE"

1834   1835

Soft as a cloud is yon blue Ridge — the Mere
Seems firm as solid crystal, breathless, clear,
And motionless; and, to the gazer's eye,
Deeper than ocean, in the immensity
Of its vague mountains and unreal sky!
But, from the process in that still retreat,
Turn to minuter changes at our feet;
Observe how dewy Twilight has withdrawn
The crowd of daisies from the shaven lawn,
And has restored to view its tender green,
That, while the sun rode high, was lost beneath
      their dazzling sheen.
— An emblem this of what the sober Hour
Can do for minds disposed to feel its power!
Thus oft, when we in vain have wished away
The petty pleasures of the garish day,
Meek eve shuts up the whole usurping host
(Unbashful dwarfs each glittering at his post)
And leaves the disencumbered spirit free
To reassume a staid simplicity.

[7]

SOFT AS A CLOUD IS YON BLUE RIDGE

'T is well — but what are helps of time and place,
When wisdom stands in need of nature's grace;
Why do good thoughts, invoked or not, descend,
Like Angels from their bowers, our virtues to befriend;
If yet To-morrow, unbelied, may say,
"I come to open out, for fresh display,
The elastic vanities of yesterday"?

"THE LEAVES THAT RUSTLED ON
THIS OAK–CROWNED HILL"

1834   1835

Composed by the side of Grasmere lake. The mountains that
enclose the vale, especially towards Easdale, are most favour-
able to the reverberation of sound. There is a passage in the
"Excursion," towards the close of the fourth book, where the
voice of the raven in flight is traced through the modifications
it undergoes, as I have often heard it in that vale and others of
this district.

> "Often, at the hour
> When issue forth the first pale stars, is heard,
> Within the circuit of this fabric huge,
> One voice — the solitary raven."

THE leaves that rustled on this oak-crowned hill,
And sky that danced among those leaves, are still;
Rest smooths the way for sleep; in field and bower
Soft shades and dews have shed their blended power
On drooping eyelid and the closing flower;
Sound is there none at which the faintest heart
Might leap, the weakest nerve of superstition start;
Save when the Owlet's unexpected scream
Pierces the ethereal vault; and ('mid the gleam
Of unsubstantial imagery, the dream,
From the hushed vale's realities, transferred

[9]

To the still lake) the imaginative Bird
Seems, 'mid inverted mountains, not unheard.
    Grave Creature! — whether, while the moon shines
        bright
On thy wings opened wide for smoothest flight,
Thou art discovered in a roofless tower,
Rising from what may once have been a lady's bower;
Or spied where thou sitt'st moping in thy mew
At the dim centre of a churchyard yew;
Or, from a rifted crag or ivy tod
Deep in a forest, thy secure abode,
Thou giv'st, for pastime's sake, by shriek or shout,
A puzzling notice of thy whereabout —
May the night never come, nor day be seen,
When I shall scorn thy voice or mock thy mien!
    In classic ages men perceived a soul
Of sapience in thy aspect, headless Owl!
Thee Athens reverenced in the studious grove;
And, near the golden sceptre grasped by Jove,
His Eagle's favourite perch, while round him sate
The Gods revolving the decrees of Fate,
Thou, too, wert present at Minerva's side: —
Hark to that second larum! — far and wide
The elements have heard, and rock and cave replied.

THE LABOURER'S NOON–DAY HYMN

1834 1835

Bishop Ken's Morning and Evening Hymns are, as they deserve to be, familiarly known. Many other hymns have also been written on the same subject; but, not being aware of any being designed for noon-day, I was induced to compose these verses. Often one has occasion to observe cottage children carrying, in their baskets, dinner to their Fathers engaged with their daily labours in the fields and woods. How gratifying would it be to me could I be assured that any portion of these stanzas had been sung by such a domestic concert under such circumstances. A friend of mine has told me that she introduced this Hymn into a village-school which she superintended, and the stanzas in succession furnished her with texts to comment upon in a way which without difficulty was made intelligible to the children, and in which they obviously took delight, and they were taught to sing it to the tune of the old 100th Psalm

Up to the throne of God is borne
The voice of praise at early morn,
And he accepts the punctual hymn
Sung as the light of day grows dim:

Nor will he turn his ear aside
From holy offerings at noontide:
Then here reposing let us raise
A song of gratitude and praise.

[11]

THE LABOURER'S NOON–DAY HYMN

What though our burthen be not light,
We need not toil from morn to night;
The respite of the mid-day hour
Is in the thankful creature's power.

Blest are the moments, doubly blest,
That, drawn from this one hour of rest,
Are with a ready heart bestowed
Upon the service of our God!

Each field is then a hallowed spot,
An altar is in each man's cot,
A church in every grove that spreads
Its living roof above our heads.

Look up to Heaven! the industrious Sun
Already half his race hath run;
He cannot halt nor go astray,
But our immortal Spirits may.

Lord! since his rising in the East,
If we have faltered or transgressed,
Guide, from thy love's abundant source,
What yet remains of this day's course:

Help with thy grace, through life's short day,
Our upward and our downward way;
And glorify for us the west,
When we shall sink to final rest.

The Returning Labourer

THE REDBREAST

SUGGESTED IN A WESTMORELAND COTTAGE

1834   1835

Written at Rydal Mount. All our cats having been banished
the house, it was soon frequented by redbreasts. Two or three
of them, when the window was open, would come in, particu-
larly when Mrs. Wordsworth was breakfasting alone, and hop
about the table picking up the crumbs. My sister being then
confined to her room by sickness, as, dear creature, she still
is, had one that, without being caged, took up its abode with
her, and at night used to perch upon a nail from which a
picture had hung. It used to sing and fan her face with
its wings in a manner that was very touching.

DRIVEN in by Autumn's sharpening air
From half-stripped woods and pastures bare,
Brisk Robin seeks a kindlier home:
Not like a beggar is he come,
But enters as a looked-for guest,
Confiding in his ruddy breast,
As if it were a natural shield
Charged with a blazon on the field,
Due to that good and pious deed
Of which we in the Ballad read.
But pensive fancies putting by,
And wild-wood sorrows, speedily

THE REDBREAST

He plays the expert ventriloquist;
And, caught by glimpses now — now missed,
Puzzles the listener with a doubt
If the soft voice he throws about
Comes from within doors or without!
Was ever such a sweet confusion,
Sustained by delicate illusion?
He 's at your elbow — to your feeling
The notes are from the floor or ceiling;
And there 's a riddle to be guessed,
'Till you have marked his heaving chest,
And busy throat whose sink and swell,
Betray the Elf that loves to dwell
In Robin's bosom, as a chosen cell.

Heart-pleased we smile upon the Bird
If seen, and with like pleasure stirred
Commend him, when he 's only heard.
But small and fugitive our gain
Compared with *hers* who long hath lain,
With languid limbs and patient head
Reposing on a lone sick-bed;
Where now, she daily hears a strain
That cheats her of too busy cares,
Eases her pain, and helps her prayers.
And who but this dear Bird beguiled
The fever of that pale-faced Child;

THE REDBREAST

Now cooling, with his passing wing,
Her forehead, like a breeze of Spring:
Recalling now, with descant soft
Shed round her pillow from aloft,
Sweet thoughts of angels hovering nigh,
And the invisible sympathy
Of "Matthew, Mark, and Luke, and John,
Blessing the bed she lies upon"?[1]
And sometimes, just as listening ends
In slumber, with the cadence blends
A dream of that low-warbled hymn
Which old folk, fondly pleased to trim
Lamps of faith, now burning dim,
Say that the Cherubs, carved in stone,
When clouds gave way at dead of night
And the ancient church was filled with light,
Used to sing in heavenly tone,
Above and round the sacred places
They guard, with wingèd baby-faces.

Thrice happy Creature! in all lands
Nurtured by hospitable hands:
Free entrance to this cot has he,
Entrance and exit both *yet* free;
And, when the keen unruffled weather
That thus brings man and bird together,
Shall with its pleasantness be past,

THE REDBREAST

And casement closed and door made fast,
To keep at bay the howling blast,
He needs not fear the season's rage,
For the whole house is Robin's cage.
Whether the bird flit here or there,
O'er table *lilt*, or perch on chair,
Though some may frown and make a stir,
To scare him as a trespasser,
And he belike will flinch or start,
Good friends he has to take his part;
One chiefly, who with voice and look
Pleads for him from the chimney-nook,
Where sits the Dame, and wears away
Her long and vacant holiday;
With images about her heart,
Reflected from the years gone by,
On human nature's second infancy.

LINES

SUGGESTED BY A PORTRAIT FROM THE PENCIL OF
F. STONE

1834   1835

This Portrait has hung for many years in our principal sit-
ting-room, and represents J. Q. as she was when a girl. The
picture, though it is somewhat thinly painted, has much
merit in tone and general effect: it is chiefly valuable, however,
from the sentiment that pervades it. The Anecdote of the
saying of the Monk in sight of Titian's picture was told in this
house by Mr. Wilkie, and was, I believe, first communicated
to the public in this poem, the former portion of which I was
composing at the time. Southey heard the story from Miss
Hutchinson, and transferred it to the "Doctor"; but it is not
easy to explain how my friend Mr. Rogers, in a note subse-
quently added to his "Italy," was led to speak of the same re-
markable words having many years before been spoken in his
hearing by a monk or priest in front of a picture of the Last
Supper, placed over a Refectory-table in a convent at Padua.

BEGUILED into forgetfulness of care
Due to the day's unfinished task; of pen
Or book regardless, and of that fair scene
In Nature's prodigality displayed
Before my window, often times and long
I gaze upon a Portrait whose mild gleam
Of beauty never ceases to enrich

[17]

The common light; whose stillness charms the air,
Or seems to charm it, into like repose;
Whose silence, for the pleasure of the ear,
Surpasses sweetest music. There she sits
With emblematic purity attired
In a white vest, white as her marble neck
Is, and the pillar of the throat would be
But for the shadow by the drooping chin
Cast into that recess — the tender shade,
The shade and light, both there and everywhere,
And through the very atmosphere she breathes,
Broad, clear, and toned harmoniously, with skill
That might from nature have been learnt in the hour
When the lone shepherd sees the morning spread
Upon the mountains. Look at her, whoe'er
Thou be that, kindling with a poet's soul,
Hast loved the painter's true Promethean craft
Intensely — from Imagination take
The treasure, — what mine eyes behold, see thou,
Even though the Atlantic ocean roll between.

A silver line, that runs from brow to crown
And in the middle parts the braided hair,
Just serves to show how delicate a soil
The golden harvest grows in; and those eyes,
Soft and capacious as a cloudless sky
Whose azure depth their colour emulates,

LINES SUGGESTED BY A PORTRAIT

Must needs be conversant with upward looks,
Prayer's voiceless service; but now, seeking nought
And shunning nought, their own peculiar life
Of motion they renounce, and with the head
Partake its inclination towards earth
In humble grace, and quiet pensiveness
Caught at the point where it stops short of sadness.
    Offspring of soul-bewitching Art, make me
Thy confidant! say, whence derived that air
Of calm abstraction? Can the ruling thought
Be with some lover far away, or one
Crossed by misfortune, or of doubted faith?
Inapt conjecture! Childhood here, a moon
Crescent in simple loveliness serene,
Has but approached the gates of womanhood,
Not entered them; her heart is yet unpierced
By the blind Archer-god; her fancy free:
The fount of feeling if unsought elsewhere,
Will not be found.
                    Her right hand, as it lies
Across the slender wrist of the left arm
Upon her lap reposing, holds — but mark
How slackly, for the absent mind permits
No firmer grasp — a little wild-flower, joined
As in a posy, with a few pale ears
Of yellowing corn, the same that overtopped

LINES SUGGESTED BY A PORTRAIT

And In their common birthplace sheltered it
Till they were plucked together; a blue flower
Called by the thrifty husbandman a weed;
But Ceres, in her garland, might have worn
That ornament, unblamed. The floweret, held
In scarcely conscious fingers, was, she knows,
(Her Father told her so) in youth's gay dawn
Her Mother's favourite; and the orphan Girl,
In her own dawn — a dawn less gay and bright,
Loves it, while there in solitary peace
She sits, for that departed Mother's sake.
— Not from a source less sacred is derived
(Surely I do not err) that pensive air
Of calm abstraction through the face diffused
And the whole person.
                              Words have something told
More than the pencil can, and verily
More than is needed, but the precious Art
Forgives their interference — Art divine,
That both creates and fixes, in despite
Of Death and Time, the marvels it hath wrought.
   Strange contrasts have we in this world of ours!
That posture, and the look of filial love
Thinking of past and gone, with what is left
Dearly united, might be swept away
From this fair Portrait's fleshly Archetype,

LINES SUGGESTED BY A PORTRAIT

Even by an innocent fancy's slightest freak
Banished, nor ever, haply, be restored
To their lost place, or meet in harmony
So exquisite; but *here* do they abide,
Ensbrined for ages. Is not then the Art
Godlike, a humble branch of the divine,
In visible quest of immortality,
Stretched forth with trembling hope? — In every
    realm,
From high Gibraltar to Siberian plains,
Thousands, in each variety of tongue
That Europe knows, would echo this appeal;
One above all, a Monk who waits on God
In the magnific Convent built of yore
To sanctify the Escurial palace. He —
Guiding, from cell to cell and room to room,
A British Painter (eminent for truth
In character, and depth of feeling, shown
By labours that have touched the hearts of kings,
And are endeared to simple cottagers) —
Came, in that service, to a glorious work,
Our Lord's Last Supper, beautiful as when first
The appropriate Picture, fresh from Titian's hand,
Graced the Refectory: and there, while both
Stood with eyes fixed upon that masterpiece,
The hoary Father in the Stranger's ear

LINES SUGGESTED BY A PORTRAIT

Breathed out these words: — "Here daily do we sit,
Thanks given to God for daily bread, and here
Pondering the mischiefs of these restless times,
And thinking of my Brethren, dead, dispersed,
Or changed and changing, I not seldom gaze
Upon this solemn Company unmoved
By shock of circumstance, or lapse of years,
Until I cannot but believe that they —
They are in truth the Substance, we the Shadows."
   So spake the mild Jeronymite, his griefs
Melting away within him like a dream
Ere he had ceased to gaze, perhaps to speak :
And I, grown old, but in a happier land,
Domestic Portrait! have to verse consigned
In thy calm presence those heart-moving words:
Words that can soothe, more than they agitate;
Whose spirit, like the angel that went down
Into Bethesda's pool, with healing virtue
Informs the fountain in the human breast
Which by the visitation was disturbed.
   — But why this stealing tear? Companion mute,
On thee I look, not sorrowing; fare thee well,
My Song's Inspirer, once again farewell![2]

THE FOREGOING SUBJECT RESUMED

1834   1835

AMONG a grave fraternity of Monks,
For One, but surely not for One alone,
Triumphs, in that great work, the Painter's skill,
Humbling the body, to exalt the soul;
Yet representing, amid wreck and wrong
And dissolution and decay, the warm
And breathing life of flesh, as if already
Clothed with impassive majesty, and graced
With no mean earnest of a heritage
Assigned to it in future worlds. Thou, too,
With thy memorial flower, meek Portraiture!
From whose serene companionship I passed
Pursued by thoughts that haunt me still; thou
          also —
Though but a simple object, into light
Called forth by those affections that endear
The private hearth; though keeping thy sole seat
In singleness, and little tried by time,
Creation, as it were, of yesterday —
With a congenial function art endued
For each and all of us, together joined

THE FOREGOING SUBJECT RESUMED

In course of nature under a low roof
By charities and duties that proceed
Out of the bosom of a wiser vow.
To a like salutary sense of awe
Or sacred wonder, growing with the power
Of meditation that attempts to weigh,
In faithful scales, things and their opposites,
Can thy enduring quiet gently raise
A household small and sensitive, — whose love,
Dependent as in part its blessings are
Upon frail ties dissolving or dissolved
On earth, will be revived, we trust, in heaven.[3]

TO A CHILD

WRITTEN IN HER ALBUM

1834 1835

This quatrain was extempore on observing this image, as I had often done, on the lawn of Rydal Mount. It was first written down in the Album of my God-daughter, Rotha Quillinan.

SMALL service is true service while it lasts:
Of humblest Friends, bright Creature! scorn not
    one:
The Daisy, by the shadow that it casts,
Protects the lingering dew-drop from the Sun.

LINES

WRITTEN IN THE ALBUM OF THE COUNTESS OF
LONSDALE.   NOV. 5, 1834

1834   1835

This is a faithful picture of that amiable Lady, as she then
was. The youthfulness of figure and demeanour and habits,
which she retained in almost unprecedented degree, departed
a very few years after, and she died without violent disease by
gradual decay before she reached the period of old age.

LADY! a Pen (perhaps with thy regard,
Among the Favoured, favoured not the least)
Left, 'mid the Records of this Book inscribed,
Deliberate traces, registers of thought
And feeling, suited to the place and time
That gave them birth: — months passed, and still this
      hand
That had not been too timid to imprint
Words which the virtues of thy Lord inspired,
Was yet not bold enough to write of Thee.
And why that scrupulous reserve? In sooth
The blameless cause lay in the Theme itself.
Flowers are there many that delight to strive
With the sharp wind, and seem to court the shower,
Yet are by nature careless of the sun

Whether he shine on them or not; and some,
Where'er he moves along the unclouded sky,
Turn a broad front full on his flattering beams:
Others do rather from their notice shrink,
Loving the dewy shade, — a humble band,
Modest and sweet, a progeny of earth,
Congenial with thy mind and character,
High-born Augusta!

        Witness, Towers and Groves!
And Thou, wild Stream, that giv'st the honoured name
Of Lowther to this ancient Line, bear witness
From thy most secret haunts; and ye Parterres,
Which She is pleased and proud to call her own,
Witness how oft upon my noble Friend
Mute offerings, tribute from an inward sense
Of admiration and respectful love,
Have waited — till the affections could no more
Endure that silence, and broke out in song,
Snatches of music taken up and dropt
Like those self-solacing, those under, notes
Trilled by the redbreast, when autumnal leaves
Are thin upon the bough. Mine, only mine,
The pleasure was, and no one heard the praise,
Checked, in the moment of its issue, checked
And reprehended, by a fancied blush
From the pure qualities that called it forth.

Thus Virtue lives debarred from Virtue's meed;
Thus, Lady, is retiredness a veil
That, while it only spreads a softening charm
O'er features looked at by discerning eyes,
Hides half their beauty from the common gaze;
And thus, even on the exposed and breezy hill
Of lofty station, female goodness walks,
When side by side with lunar gentleness,
As in a cloister. Yet the grateful Poor
(Such the immunities of low estate,
Plain Nature's enviable privilege,
Her sacred recompense for many wants)
Open their hearts before Thee, pouring out
All that they think and feel, with tears of joy;
And benedictions not unheard in heaven
And friend in the ear of friend, where speech is free
To follow truth, is eloquent as they.

Then let the Book receive in these prompt lines
A just memorial; and thine eyes consent
To read that they, who mark thy course, behold
A life declining with the golden light
Of summer, in the season of sere leaves;
See cheerfulness undamped by stealing Time;
See studied kindness flow with easy stream,
Illustrated with inborn courtesy;
And an habitual disregard of self

LINES WRITTEN IN AN ALBUM

Balanced by vigilance for others' weal.
  And shall the Verse not tell of lighter gifts
With these ennobling attributes conjoined
And blended, in peculiar harmony,
By Youth's surviving spirit? What agile grace!
A nymph-like liberty, in nymph-like form,
Beheld with wonder; whether floor or path
Thou tread; or sweep — borne on the managed steed
Fleet as the shadows, over down or field,
Driven by strong winds at play among the clouds.
  Yet one word more — one farewell word — a wish
Which came, but it has passed into a prayer —
That, as thy sun in brightness is declining,
So — at an hour yet distant for *their* sakes
Whose tender love, here faltering on the way
Of a diviner love, will be forgiven —
So may it set in peace, to rise again
For everlasting glory won by faith.

TO THE MOON

COMPOSED BY THE SEASIDE, — ON THE COAST OF
CUMBERLAND

1835   1836

WANDERER! that stoop'st so low, and com'st so near
To human life's unsettled atmosphere;
Who lov'st with Night and Silence to partake,
So might it seem, the cares of them that wake;
And, through the cottage-lattice softly peeping,
Dost shield from harm the humblest of the sleeping;
What pleasure once encompassed those sweet names
Which yet in thy behalf the Poet claims,
An idolizing dreamer as of yore! —
I slight them all; and, on this sea-beat shore
Sole-sitting, only can to thoughts attend
That bid me hail thee as the SAILOR'S FRIEND;
So call thee for heaven's grace through thee made known
By confidence supplied and mercy shown,
When not a twinkling star or beacon's light
Abates the perils of a stormy night;
And for less obvious benefits, that find
Their way, with thy pure help, to heart and mind;
Both for the adventurer starting in life's prime;
And veteran ranging round from clime to clime,

[30]

TO THE MOON

Long-baffled hope's slow fever in his veins,
And wounds and weakness oft his labour's sole remains
   The aspiring Mountains and the winding Streams,
Empress of Night! are gladdened by thy beams;
A look of thine the wilderness pervades,
And penetrates the forest's inmost shades;
Thou, chequering peaceably the minster's gloom,
Guid'st the pale Mourner to the lost one's tomb;
Canst reach the Prisoner — to his grated cell
Welcome, though silent and intangible! —
And lives there one, of all that come and go
On the great waters toiling to and fro,
One, who has watched thee at some quiet hour
Enthroned aloft in undisputed power,
Or crossed by vapoury streaks and clouds that move
Catching the lustre they in part reprove —
Nor sometimes felt a fitness in thy sway
To call up thoughts that shun the glare of day,
And make the serious happier than the gay?

   Yes, lovely Moon! if thou so mildly bright
Dost rouse, yet surely in thy own despite,
To fiercer mood the phrenzy-stricken brain,
Let me a compensating faith maintain;
That there 's a sensitive, a tender, part
Which thou canst touch in every human heart,
For healing and composure. — But, as least

TO THE MOON

And mightiest billows ever have confessed
Thy domination; as the whole vast Sea
Feels through her lowest depths thy sovereignty;
So shines that countenance with especial grace
On them who urge the keel her *plains* to trace
Furrowing its way right onward. The most rude,
Cut off from home and country, may have stood —
Even till long gazing hath bedimmed his eye,
Or the mute rapture ended in a sigh —
Touched by accordance of thy placid cheer,
With some internal lights to memory dear,
Or fancies stealing forth to soothe the breast
Tired with its daily share of earth's unrest, —
Gentle awakenings, visitations meek;
A kindly influence whereof few will speak,
Though it can wet with tears the hardiest cheek.

   And when thy beauty in the shadowy cave
Is hidden, buried in its monthly grave;
Then, while the Sailor, 'mid an open sea
Swept by a favouring wind that leaves thought free,
Paces the deck — no star perhaps in sight,
And nothing save the moving ship's own light
To cheer the long dark hours of vacant night —
Oft with his musings does thy image blend,
In his mind's eye thy crescent horns ascend,
And thou art still, O Moon, that SAILOR'S FRIEND!

TO THE MOON

RYDAL

1835 1836

QUEEN of the stars! — so gentle, so benign,
That ancient Fable did to thee assign,
When darkness creeping o'er thy silver brow
Warned thee these upper regions to forego,
Alternate empire in the shades below —
A Bard, who, lately near the wide-spread sea
Traversed by gleaming ships, looked up to thee
With grateful thoughts, doth now thy rising hail
From the close confines of a shadowy vale.
Glory of night, conspicuous yet serene,
Nor less attractive when by glimpses seen
Through cloudy umbrage, well might that fair face,
And all those attributes of modest grace,
In days when Fancy wrought unchecked by fear,
Down to the green earth fetch thee from thy sphere,
To sit in leafy woods by fountains clear!
  O still beloved (for thine, meek Power, are charms
That fascinate the very Babe in arms,
While he, uplifted towards thee, laughs outright,
Spreading his little palms in his glad Mother's sight)

[33]

TO THE MOON

O still beloved, once worshipped! Time, that frowns
In his destructive flight on earthly crowns,
Spares thy mild splendour; still those far-shot beams
Tremble on dancing waves and rippling streams
With stainless touch, as chaste as when thy praise
Was sung by Virgin-choirs in festal lays;
And through dark trials still dost thou explore
Thy way for increase punctual as of yore,
When teeming Matrons — yielding to rude faith
In mysteries of birth and life and death
And painful struggle and deliverance — prayed
Of thee to visit them with lenient aid.
What though the rites be swept away, the fanes
Extinct that echoed to the votive strains;
Yet thy mild aspect does not, cannot, cease
Love to promote and purity and peace;
And Fancy, unreproved, even yet may trace
Faint types of suffering in thy beamless face.
  Then, silent Monitress! let us — not blind
To worlds unthought of till the searching mind
Of Science laid them open to mankind —
Told, also, how the voiceless heavens declare
God's glory; and acknowledging thy share
In that blest charge; let us — without offence
To aught of highest, holiest influence —
Receive whatever good 't is given thee to dispense.

TO THE MOON

May sage and simple, catching with one eye
The moral intimations of the sky,
Learn from thy course, where'er their own be taken,
"To look on tempests, and be never shaken";
To keep with faithful step the appointed way,
Eclipsing or eclipsed, by night or day,
And from example of thy monthly range
Gently to brook decline and fatal change;
Meek, patient, stedfast, and with loftier scope,
Than thy revival yields, for gladsome hope!

WRITTEN AFTER THE DEATH OF CHARLES LAMB

1835   1836

Light will be thrown upon the tragic circumstance alluded to in this poem when, after the death of Charles Lamb's Sister, his biographer, Mr. Sergeant Talfourd, shall be at liberty to relate particulars which could not, at the time his Memoir was written, be given to the public. Mary Lamb was ten years older than her brother, and has survived him as long a time. Were I to give way to my own feelings, I should dwell not only on her genius and intellectual powers, but upon the delicacy and refinement of manner which she maintained inviolable under most trying circumstances. She was loved and honoured by all her brother's friends; and others, some of them strange characters, whom his philanthropic peculiarities induced him to countenance. The death of C. Lamb himself was doubtless hastened by his sorrow for that of Coleridge, to whom he had been attached from the time of their being school-fellows at Christ's Hospital. Lamb was a good Latin scholar, and probably would have gone to college upon one of the school foundations but for the impediment in his speech. Had such been his lot, he would most likely have been preserved from the indulgences of social humours and fancies which were often injurious to himself, and causes of severe regret to his friends, without really benefiting the object of his misapplied kindness.

To a good man of most dear memory
This Stone is sacred. Here he lies apart
From the great city where he first drew breath,
Was reared and taught; and humbly earned his bread,

AFTER THE DEATH OF C. LAMB

To the strict labours of the merchant's desk
By duty chained. Not seldom did those tasks
Tease, and the thought of time so spent depress,
His spirit, but the recompence was high;
Firm Independence, Bounty's rightful sire;
Affections, warm as sunshine, free as air;
And when the precious hours of leisure came,
Knowledge and wisdom, gained from converse sweet
With books, or while he ranged the crowded streets
With a keen eye, and overflowing heart:
So genius triumphed over seeming wrong,
And poured out truth in works by thoughtful love
Inspired — works potent over smiles and tears.
And as round mountain-tops the lightning plays,
Thus innocently sported, breaking forth
As from a cloud of some grave sympathy,
Humour and wild instinctive wit, and all
The vivid flashes of his spoken words.
From the most gentle creature nursed in fields [4]
Had been derived the name he bore — a name,
Wherever Christian altars have been raised,
Hallowed to meekness and to innocence;
And if in him meekness at times gave way,
Provoked out of herself by troubles strange,
Many and strange, that hung about his life;
Still, at the centre of his being, lodged

AFTER THE DEATH OF C. LAMB

A soul by resignation sanctified:
And if too often, self-reproached, he felt
That innocence belongs not to our kind,
A power that never ceased to abide in him,
Charity, 'mid the multitude of sins
That she can cover, left not his exposed
To an unforgiving judgment from just Heaven.
Oh, he was good, if e'er a good Man lived!

.   .   .   .

From a reflecting mind and sorrowing heart
Those simple lines flowed with an earnest wish,
Though but a doubting hope, that they might serve
Fitly to guard the precious dust of him
Whose virtues called them forth. That aim is missed;
    For much that truth most urgently required
Had from a faltering pen been asked in vain:
Yet, haply, on the printed page received,
The imperfect record, there, may stand unblamed
As long as verse of mine shall breathe the air
Of memory, or see the light of love.
    Thou wert a scorner of the fields, my Friend,
But more in show than truth; and from the fields,
And from the mountains, to thy rural grave
Transported, my soothed spirit hovers o'er
Its green untrodden turf, and blowing flowers;
And taking up a voice shall speak (tho' still

AFTER THE DEATH OF C. LAMB

Awed by the theme's peculiar sanctity
Which words less free presumed not even to touch)
Of that fraternal love, whose heaven-lit lamp
From infancy, through manhood, to the last
Of threescore years, and to thy latest hour,
Burnt on with ever-strengthening light, enshrined
Within thy bosom.
           "Wonderful" hath been
The love established between man and man,
"Passing the love of women"; and between
Man and his help-mate in fast wedlock joined
Through God, is raised a spirit and soul of love
Without whose blissful influence Paradise
Had been no Paradise; and earth were now
A waste where creatures bearing human form,
Direst of savage beasts, would roam in fear,
Joyless and comfortless. Our days glide on;
And let him grieve who cannot choose but grieve
That he hath been an Elm without his Vine,
And her bright dower of clustering charities,
That, round his trunk and branches, might have clung
Enriching and adorning. Unto thee,
Not so enriched, not so adorned, to thee
Was given (say rather, thou of later birth
Wert given to her) a Sister — 't is a word
Timidly uttered, for she *lives*, the meek,

The self-restraining, and the ever-kind;
In whom thy reason and intelligent heart
Found — for all interests, hopes, and tender cares,
All softening, humanising, hallowing powers,
Whether withheld, or for her sake unsought —
More than sufficient recompence!
                              Her love
(What weakness prompts the voice to tell it here?)
Was as the love of mothers; and when years,
Lifting the boy to man's estate, had called
The long-protected to assume the part
Of a protector, the first filial tie
Was undissolved; and, in or out of sight,
Remained imperishably interwoven
With life itself. Thus, 'mid a shifting world,
Did they together testify of time
And season's difference — a double tree
With two collateral stems sprung from one root;
Such were they — such thro' life they *might* have been
In union, in partition only such;
Otherwise wrought the will of the Most High;
Yet, thro' all visitations and all trials,
Still they were faithful; like two vessels launched
From the same beach one ocean to explore
With mutual help, and sailing — to their league
True, as inexorable winds, or bars

AFTER THE DEATH OF C. LAMB

Floating or fixed of polar ice, allow.
  But turn we rather, let my spirit turn
With thine, O silent and invisible Friend!
To those dear intervals, nor rare nor brief,
When reunited, and by choice withdrawn
From miscellaneous converse, ye were taught
That the remembrance of foregone distress,
And the worse fear of future ill (which oft
Doth hang around it, as a sickly child
Upon its mother) may be both alike
Disarmed of power to unsettle present good
So prized, and things inward and outward held
In such an even balance, that the heart
Acknowledges God's grace, his mercy feels,
And in its depth of gratitude is still.
  O gift divine of quiet sequestration!
The hermit, exercised in prayer and praise,
And feeding daily on the hope of heaven,
Is happy in his vow, and fondly cleaves
To life-long singleness; but happier far
Was to your souls, and, to the thoughts of others,
A thousand times more beautiful appeared,
Your *dual* loneliness. The sacred tie
Is broken; yet why grieve? for Time but holds
His moiety in trust, till Joy shall lead
To the blest world where parting is unknown.

EXTEMPORE EFFUSION UPON THE DEATH OF JAMES HOGG

1835   1836

These verses were written extempore, immediately after
reading a notice of the Ettrick Shepherd's death in the New-
castle paper, to the Editor of which I sent a copy for publica-
tion. The persons lamented in these verses were all either of
my friends or acquaintance. In Lockhart's *Life of Sir Walter
Scott* an account is given of my first meeting with him in 1803.
How the Ettrick Shepherd and I became known to each other
has already been mentioned in these notes. He was undoubt-
edly a man of original genius, but of coarse manners and low
and offensive opinions. Of Coleridge and Lamb I need not
speak here. Crabbe I have met in London at Mr. Rogers's,
but more frequently and favourably at Mr. Hoare's upon
Hampstead Heath. Every spring he used to pay that family a
visit of some length, and was upon terms of intimate friendship
with Mrs. Hoare, and still more with her daughter-in-law, who
has a large collection of his letters addressed to herself. After
the Poet's decease, application was made to her to give up
these letters to his biographer, that they, or at least part of
them, might be given to the public. She hesitated to comply,
and asked my opinion on the subject. "By no means," was
my answer, grounded not upon any objection there might be
to publishing a selection from these letters, but from an aver-
sion I have always felt to meet idle curiosity by calling back
the recently departed to become the object of trivial and fa-
miliar gossip. Crabbe obviously for the most part preferred
the company of women to that of men, for this among other

[42]

reasons, that he did not like to be put upon the stretch in general conversation: accordingly in miscellaneous society his *talk* was so much below what might have been expected from a man so deservedly celebrated, that to me it seemed trifling. It must upon other occasions have been of a different character, as I found in our rambles together on Hampstead Heath, and not so much from a readiness to communicate his knowledge of life and manners as of natural history in all its branches. His mind was inquisitive, and he seems to have taken refuge from the remembrance of the distresses he had gone through, in these studies and the employments to which they led. Moreover, such contemplations might tend profitably to counterbalance the painful truths which he had collected from his intercourse with mankind. Had I been more intimate with him, I should have ventured to touch upon his office as a minister of the Gospel, and how far his heart and soul were in it so as to make him a zealous and diligent labourer: in poetry, though he wrote much, as we all know, he assuredly was not so. I happened once to speak of pains as necessary to produce merit of a certain kind which I highly valued: his observation was — "It is not worth while." You are quite right, thought I, if the labour encroaches upon the time due to teach truth as a steward of the mysteries of God; if there be cause to fear *that*, write less: but, if poetry is to be produced at all, make what you do produce as good as you can. Mr. Rogers once told me that he expressed his regret to Crabbe that he wrote in his later works so much less correctly than in his earlier. "Yes," replied he, "but then I had a reputation to make; now I can afford to relax." Whether it was from a modest estimate of his own qualifications, or from causes less creditable, his motives for writing verse and his hopes and aims were not so high as is to be desired. After being silent for more than twenty years, he again applied himself to poetry, upon the spur of applause he received from the periodical publications of the day, as he himself tells us in one of his prefaces. Is it not to be lamented that a man who was so conversant with permanent truth, and whose writings are so valuable an acquisition to our country's literature, should have *required* an impulse from such a quarter? — Mrs. Hemans was unfortunate as a poetess in being obliged by circumstances to write for money, and that so frequently and so much, that she was compelled to look out for subjects wherever she could find them, and to write as expeditiously as possible. As a woman, she was to a considerable degree a spoilt child of the world. She had been early in life distinguished for talent, and poems of hers were published while she was a girl. She had also been handsome in her youth, but her education had been most unfortunate. She was totally ignorant of housewifery, and could as easily have managed the spear of Minerva as her needle. It was from observing these deficiencies, that, one day while she was under my roof, I *purposely* directed her attention to household economy, and told her I had purchased *Scales*, which I intended to present to a young lady as a wedding present; pointed out their utility (for her especial benefit), and said that no *ménage* ought to be without them. Mrs. Hemans, not in the least suspecting my drift, reported this saying, in a letter to a friend at the time, as a proof of my simplicity. Being disposed to make large allowances for the faults of her education and the circumstances in which she was placed, I felt most kindly disposed towards her, and took her part upon all occasions, and I was not a little affected by learning that after she withdrew to Ireland, a long and severe sickness raised her spirit as it depressed her body. This I heard from her most intimate friends, and there is striking evidence of it in a poem written and published not long before her death. These notices of Mrs. Hemans would be very unsatisfactory to her intimate friends, as indeed they are to myself, not so much for what is said, but what for brevity's sake is left unsaid. Let it suffice to add, there was much sympathy between us, and, if opportunity had been allowed me to see more of her, I should have loved and valued her accordingly; as it is, I remember her with true affection for her amiable qualities, and, above all, for her delicate and irreproachable conduct during her long separation from an unfeeling husband, whom she had been led to marry from the romantic notions of inexperienced youth. Upon this husband I never heard her cast the least reproach, nor did I ever hear her even name him, though she did not wholly forbear to touch upon her domestic position; but never so as that any fault could be found with her manner of adverting to it.

WHEN first, descending from the moorlands,
I saw the Stream of Yarrow glide
Along a bare and open valley,
The Ettrick Shepherd was my guide.

When last along its banks I wandered,
Through groves that had begun to shed
Their golden leaves upon the pathways,
My steps the Border-minstrel led.

The mighty Minstrel breathes no longer,
'Mid mouldering ruins low he lies;
And death upon the braes of Yarrow,
Has closed the Shepherd-poet's eyes:

Nor has the rolling year twice measured,
From sign to sign, its stedfast course,
Since every mortal power of Coleridge
Was frozen at its marvellous source;

UPON THE DEATH OF JAMES HOGG

The rapt One, of the godlike forehead,
The heaven-eyed creature sleeps in earth:
And Lamb, the frolic and the gentle,
Has vanished from his lonely hearth.

Like clouds that rake the mountain-summits,
Or waves that own no curbing hand,
How fast has brother followed brother
From sunshine to the sunless land!

Yet I, whose lids from infant slumber
Were earlier raised, remain to hear
A timid voice, that asks in whispers,
"Who next will drop and disappear?"

Our haughty life is crowned with darkness,
Like London with its own black wreath,
On which with thee, O Crabbe! forth-looking,
I gazed from Hampstead's breezy heath.

As if but yesterday departed,
Thou too art gone before; but why,
O'er ripe fruit, seasonably gathered,
Should frail survivors heave a sigh?

Mourn rather for that holy Spirit,
Sweet as the spring, as ocean deep;

UPON THE DEATH OF JAMES HOGG

For Her, who, ere her summer faded,
Has sunk into a breathless sleep.

No more of old romantic sorrows,
For slaughtered Youth or love-lorn Maid!
With sharper grief is Yarrow smitten,
And Ettrick mourns with her their Poet dead.[5]

UPON SEEING A COLOURED DRAWING OF THE BIRD OF PARADISE IN AN ALBUM

1835 1836

I cannot forbear to record that the last seven lines of this Poem were composed in bed during the night of the day on which my sister Sara Hutchinson died about 6 P. M., and it was the thought of her innocent and beautiful life that, through faith, prompted the words —

"On wings that fear no glance of God's pure sight,
No tempest from his breath."

The reader will find two poems on pictures of this bird among my Poems. I will here observe that in a far greater number of instances than have been mentioned in these notes one poem has, as in this case, grown out of another, either because I felt the subject had been inadequately treated, or that the thoughts and images suggested in course of composition have been such as I found interfered with the unity indispensable to every work of art, however humble in character.

WHO rashly strove thy Image to portray?
Thou buoyant minion of the tropic air;
How could he think of the live creature — gay
With a divinity of colours, drest
In all her brightness, from the dancing crest
Far as the last gleam of the filmy train
Extended and extending to sustain

THE BIRD OF PARADISE

The motions that it graces — and forbear
To drop his pencil! Flowers of every clime
Depicted on these pages smile at time;
And gorgeous insects copied with nice care
Are here, and likenesses of many a shell
Tossed ashore by restless waves,
Or in the diver's grasp fetched up from caves
Where sea-nymphs might be proud to dwell:
But whose rash hand (again I ask) could dare,
'Mid casual tokens and promiscuous shows,
To circumscribe this Shape in fixed repose;
Could imitate for indolent survey,
Perhaps for touch profane,
Plumes that might catch, but cannot keep, a stain;
And, with cloud-streaks lightest and loftiest, share
The sun's first greeting, his last farewell ray!

Resplendent Wanderer! followed with glad eyes
Where'er her course; mysterious Bird!
To whom, by wondering Fancy stirred,
Eastern Islanders have given
A holy name — the Bird of Heaven!
And even a title higher still,
The Bird of God! whose blessed will
She seems performing as she flies
Over the earth and through the skies
In never-wearied search of Paradise —

[49]

THE BIRD OF PARADISE

Region that crowns her beauty with the name
She bears for *us* — for us how blest,
How happy at all seasons, could like aim
Uphold our Spirits urged to kindred flight
On wings that fear no glance of God's pure sight,
No tempest from his breath, their promised rest
Seeking with indefatigable quest
Above a world that deems itself most wise
When most enslaved by gross realities!

"BY A BLEST HUSBAND GUIDED, MARY CAME"

1835   1835

This lady was named Carleton; she, along with a sister, was brought up in the neighbourhood of Ambleside. The epitaph, a part of it at least, is in the church at Bromsgrove, where she resided after her marriage.

By a blest Husband guided, Mary came
From nearest kindred, Vernon her new name;
She came, though meek of soul, in seemly pride
Of happiness and hope, a youthful Bride.
O dread reverse! if aught *be* so, which proves
That God will chasten whom he dearly loves.
Faith bore her up through pains in mercy given,
And troubles that were each a step to Heaven:
Two Babes were laid in earth before she died;
A third now slumbers at the Mother's side;
Its Sister-twin survives, whose smiles afford
A trembling solace to her widowed Lord.

Reader! if to thy bosom cling the pain
Of recent sorrow combated in vain;
Or if thy cherished grief have failed to thwart
Time still intent on his insidious part,
Lulling the mourner's best good thoughts asleep,

BY A BLEST HUSBAND GUIDED

Pilfering regrets we would, but cannot, keep;
Bear with Him— judge *Him* gently who makes
    known
His bitter loss by this memorial Stone;
And pray that in his faithful breast the grace
Of resignation find a hallowed place.

SONNETS

I

1835(?)   1835

DESPONDING Father! mark this altered bough,
So beautiful of late, with sunshine warmed,
Or moist with dews; what more unsightly now,
Its blossoms shrivelled, and its fruit, if formed,
Invisible? yet Spring her genial brow
Knits not o'er that discolouring and decay
As false to expectation. Nor fret thou
At like unlovely process in the May
Of human life; a Stripling's graces blow,
Fade and are shed, that from their timely fall
(Misdeem it not a cankerous change) may grow
Rich mellow bearings, that for thanks shall call:
In all men, sinful is it to be slow
To hope — in Parents, sinful above all.

SONNETS

II

ROMAN ANTIQUITIES DISCOVERED AT BISHOPSTONE, HEREFORDSHIRE

1835(?)   1835

My attention to these antiquities was directed by Mr.
Walker, son to the itinerant Eidouranian Philosopher. The
beautiful pavement was discovered within a few yards of the
front door of his parsonage, and appeared from the site (in full
view of several hills upon which there had formerly been Ro-
man encampments) as if it might have been the villa of the
commander of the forces, at least such was Mr. Walker's con-
jecture.

WHILE poring Antiquarians search the ground
Upturned with curious pains, the Bard, a Seer,
Takes fire: — The men that have been reappear;
Romans for travel girt, for business gowned;
And some recline on couches, myrtle-crowned,
In festal glee: why not? For fresh and clear,
As if its hues were of the passing year,
Dawns this time-buried pavement. From that mound
Hoards may come forth of Trajans, Maximins,
Shrunk into coins with all their warlike toil:
Or a fierce impress issues with its foil
Of tenderness — the Wolf, whose suckling Twins
The unlettered ploughboy pities when he wins
The casual treasure from the furrowed soil.

SONNETS

III

ST. CATHERINE OF LEDBURY

1835(?)   1835

Written on a journey from Brinsop Court, Herefordshire.

WHEN human touch (as monkish books attest)
Nor was applied nor could be, Ledbury bells
Broke forth in concert flung adown the dells,
And upward, high as Malvern's cloudy crest;
Sweet tones, and caught by a noble Lady blest
To rapture! Mabel listened at the side
Of her loved mistress: soon the music died,
And Catherine said, 𝔥𝔢𝔯𝔢 𝔍 𝔰𝔢𝔱 𝔲𝔭 𝔪𝔶 𝔯𝔢𝔰𝔱.
Warned in a dream, the Wanderer long had sought
A home that by such miracle of sound
Must be revealed: — she heard it now, or felt
The deep, deep joy of a confiding thought;
And there, a saintly Anchoress, she dwelt
Till she exchanged for heaven that happy ground.

SONNETS

IV

1835(?)   1835

In the month of January, when Dora and I were walking
from Town-end, Grasmere, across the vale, snow being on the
ground, she espied, in the thick though leafless hedge, a bird's
nest half filled with snow. Out of this comfortless appearance
arose this Sonnet, which was, in fact, written without the least
reference to any individual object, but merely to prove to my-
self that I could, if I thought fit, write in a strain that Poets
have been fond of. On the 14th of February in the same year,
my daughter, in a sportive mood, sent it as a Valentine, under
a fictitious name, to her cousin C. W.

WHY art thou silent! Is thy love a plant
Of such weak fibre that the treacherous air
Of absence withers what was once so fair?
Is there no debt to pay, no boon to grant?
Yet have my thoughts for thee been vigilant —
Bound to thy service with unceasing care,
The mind's least generous wish a mendicant
For nought but what thy happiness could spare.
Speak — though this soft warm heart, once free to hold
A thousand tender pleasures, thine and mine,
Be left more desolate, more dreary cold
Than a forsaken bird's-nest filled with snow
'Mid its own bush of leafless eglantine —
Speak, that my torturing doubts their end may know!

[56]

SONNETS

V

1835(?)   1835

Suggested on the road between Preston and Lancaster
where it first gives a view of the Lake country, and composed
on the same day, on the roof of the coach.

FOUR fiery steeds impatient of the rein
Whirled us o'er sunless ground beneath a sky
As void of sunshine, when, from that wide plain,
Clear tops of far-off mountains we descry,
Like a Sierra of cerulean Spain,
All light and lustre. Did no heart reply?
Yes, there was One; — for One, asunder fly
The thousand links of that ethereal chain;
And green vales open out, with grove and field,
And the fair front of many a happy Home;
Such tempting spots as into vision come
While Soldiers, weary of the arms they wield
And sick at heart of strifeful Christendom,
Gaze on the moon by parting clouds revealed.

VI

TO ——

1835(?) 1835

The fate of this poor Dove, as described, was told to me at
Brinsop Court, by the young lady to whom I have given the
name of Lesbia.

> " Miss not the occasion: by the forelock take
> That subtile Power, the never-halting Time,
> Lest a mere moment's putting-off should make
> Mischance almost as heavy as a crime."

"WAIT, prithee, wait!" this answer Lesbia threw
Forth to her Dove, and took no further heed;
Her eye was busy, while her fingers flew
Across the harp, with soul-engrossing speed;
But from that bondage when her thoughts were freed
She rose, and toward the close-shut casement drew,
Whence the poor unregarded Favourite, true
To old affections, had been heard to plead
With flapping wing for entrance. What a shriek!
Forced from that voice so lately tuned to a strain
Of harmony! — a shriek of terror, pain,
And self-reproach! for, from aloft, a Kite
Pounced, — and the Dove, which from its ruthless beak
She could not rescue, perished in her sight!

SONNETS

VII

1835(?) 1835

SAID Secrecy to Cowardice and Fraud,
Falsehood and Treachery, in close council met,
Deep under ground, in Pluto's cabinet,
"The frost of England's pride will soon be thawed;
Hooded the open brow that overawed
Our schemes; the faith and honour, never yet
By us with hope encountered, be upset; —
For once I burst my bands, and cry, applaud!"
Then whispered she, "The Bill is carrying out!"
They heard, and, starting up, the Brood of Night
Clapped hands, and shook with glee their matted locks;
All Powers and Places that abhor the light
Joined in the transport, echoed back their shout,
Hurrah for ——, hugging his Ballot-box!

[59]

NOVEMBER 1836

1836   1837

EVEN so for me a Vision sanctified
The sway of death; long ere mine eyes had seen
Thy countenance — the still rapture of thy mien —
When thou, dear Sister! wert become Death's Bride:
No trace of pain or languor could abide
That change: — age on thy brow was smoothed — thy
    cold
Wan cheek at once was privileged to unfold
A loveliness to living youth denied.
Oh! if within me hope should e'er decline,
The lamp of faith, lost Friend! too faintly burn;
Then may that heaven-revealing smile of thine,
The bright assurance, visibly return:
And let my spirit in that power divine
Rejoice, as, through that power, it ceased to mourn.

"SIX MONTHS TO SIX YEARS ADDED HE REMAINED"

1836   1836

Six months to six years added he remained
Upon this sinful earth, by sin unstained:
O blessed Lord! whose mercy then removed
A Child whom every eye that looked on loved;
Support us, teach us calmly to resign
What we possessed, and now is wholly thine!

MEMORIALS OF A TOUR IN ITALY

1837–42 1842

During my whole life I had felt a strong desire to visit Rome
and the other celebrated cities and regions of Italy, but did not
think myself justified in incurring the necessary expense till I
received from Mr. Moxon, the publisher of a large edition of
my poems, a sum sufficient to enable me to gratify my wish
without encroaching upon what I considered due to my family.
My excellent friend H. C. Robinson readily consented to ac-
company me, and in March 1837, we set off from London, to
which we returned in August, earlier than my companion
wished or I should myself have desired had I been, like him, a
bachelor. These Memorials of that tour touch upon but a
very few of the places and objects that interested me, and, in
what they do advert to, are for the most part much slighter
than I could wish. More particularly do I regret that there is
no notice in them of the South of France, nor of the Roman
antiquities abounding in that district, especially of the Pont
du Gard, which, together with its situation, impressed me full
as much as any remains of Roman architecture to be found
in Italy. Then there was Vaucluse, with its Fountain, its Pe-
trarch, its rocks of all seasons, its small plots of lawn in their
first vernal freshness, and the blossoms of the peach and other
trees embellishing the scene on every side. The beauty of the
stream also called forcibly for the expression of sympathy from
one who from his childhood had studied the brooks and tor-
rents of his native mountains. Between two and three hours
did I run about climbing the steep and rugged crags from
whose base the water of Vaucluse breaks forth. "Has Laura's
Lover," often said I to myself, "ever sat down upon this stone?
or has his foot ever pressed that turf?" Some, especially of the

female sex, would have felt sure of it: my answer was (impute it to my years), "I fear not." Is it not in fact obvious that many of his love verses must have flowed, I do not say from a wish to display his own talent, but from a habit of exercising his intellect in that way rather than from an impulse of his heart? It is otherwise with his Lyrical poems, and particularly with the one upon the degradation of his country: there he pours out his reproaches, lamentations, and aspirations like an ardent and sincere patriot. But enough: it is time to turn to my own effusions, such as they are.

TO

HENRY CRABB ROBINSON

Companion! by whose buoyant Spirit cheered,
In whose experience trusting, day by day
Treasures I gained with zeal that neither feared
The toils nor felt the crosses of the way,
These records take, and happy should I be
Were but the Gift a meet Return to thee
For kindnesses that never ceased to flow,
And prompt self-sacrifice to which I owe
Far more than any heart but mine can know.

W. Wordsworth.

Rydal Mount, *Feb. 14th*, 1842.

The Tour of which the following Poems are very inadequate remembrances was shortened by report, too well founded, of the prevalence of Cholera at Naples. To make some amends for what was reluctantly left unseen in the South of Italy, we visited the Tuscan Sanctuaries among the Apennines, and the principal Italian Lakes among the Alps. Neither of those lakes, nor of Venice, is there any notice in these Poems, chiefly because I have touched upon them elsewhere. See, in particular, "Descriptive Sketches," "Memorials of a Tour on the Continent in 1820," and a Sonnet upon the extinction of the Venetian Republic.

[63]

I

MUSINGS NEAR AQUAPENDENTE

April 1837   1842

> "Not the less
> Had his sunk eye kindled at those dear words
> That spake of bards and minstrels."

His, Sir Walter Scott's eye, *did* in fact kindle at them, for the lines, "Places forsaken now," and the two that follow were adopted from a poem of mine which nearly forty years ago was in part read to him, and he never forgot them.

> "Old Helvellyn's brow,
> Where once together, in his day of strength,
> We stood rejoicing."

Sir Humphry Davy was with us at the time. We had ascended from Paterdale, and I could not but admire the vigour with which Scott scrambled along that horn of the mountain called "Striding Edge." Our progress was necessarily slow, and was beguiled by Scott's telling many stories and amusing anecdotes, as was his custom. Sir H. Davy would have probably been better pleased if other topics had occasionally been interspersed, and some discussion entered upon: at all events he did not remain with us long at the top of the mountain, but left us to find our way down its steep side together into the vale of Grasmere, where, at my cottage, Mrs. Scott was to meet us at dinner.

> "With faint smile
> He said, — 'When I am there, although 't is fair,
> 'T will be another Yarrow.'"

[64]

MUSINGS NEAR AQUAPENDENTE

See among these notes the one on "Yarrow Revisited."

"A few short steps (painful they were)."

This, though introduced here, I did not know till it was told me at Rome by Miss Mackenzie of Seaforth, a lady whose friendly attentions during my residence at Rome I have gratefully acknowledged, with expressions of sincere regret that she is no more. Miss M. told me that she accompanied Sir Walter to the Janicular Mount, and, after showing him the grave of Tasso in the church upon the top, and a mural monument there erected to his memory, they left the church and stood together on the brow of the hill overlooking the city of Rome: his daughter Anne was with them, and she, naturally desirous, for the sake of Miss Mackenzie especially, to have some expression of pleasure from her father, half reproached him for showing nothing of that kind either by his looks or voice: "How can I," replied he, "having only one leg to stand upon, and that in extreme pain!" so that the prophecy was more than fulfilled.

"Over waves rough and deep."

We took boat near the lighthouse at the point of the right horn of the bay which makes a sort of natural port for Genoa; but the wind was high, and the waves long and rough, so that I did not feel quite recompensed by the view of the city, splendid as it was, for the danger apparently incurred. The boatman (I had only one) encouraged me, saying we were quite safe, but I was not a little glad when we gained the shore, though Shelley and Byron — one of them at least, who seemed to have courted agitation from any quarter — would have probably rejoiced in such a situation: more than once I believe were they both in extreme danger even on the Lake of Geneva. Every man however has his fears of some kind or other; and no doubt they had theirs: of all men whom I have ever known,

[65]

Coleridge had the most of passive courage in bodily peril, but no one was so easily cowed when moral firmness was required in miscellaneous conversation or in the daily intercourse of social life.

> "How lovely robed in forenoon light and shade,
>   Each ministering to each, didst thou appear,
>   Savona."

There is not a single bay along this beautiful coast that might not raise in a traveller a wish to take up his abode there, each as it succeeds seems more inviting than the other; but the desolated convent on the cliff in the bay of Savona struck my fancy most; and had I, for the sake of my own health or that of a dear friend, or any other cause, been desirous of a residence abroad, I should have let my thoughts loose upon a scheme of turning some part of this building into a habitation provided as far as might be with English comforts. There is close by it a row or avenue, I forget which, of tall cypresses. I could not forbear saying to myself — "What a sweet family walk, or one for lonely musings, would be found under the shade!" but there, probably, the trees remained little noticed and seldom enjoyed.

> "This flowering broom's dear neighbourhood."

The broom is a great ornament through the months of March and April to the vales and hills of the Apennines, in the wild parts of which it blows in the utmost profusion, and of course successively at different elevations as the season advances. It surpasses ours in beauty and fragrance, but, speaking from my own limited observation only, I cannot affirm the same of several of their wild spring flowers, the primroses in particular, which I saw not unfrequently but thinly scattered and languishing compared to ours.

The note at the close of this poem, upon the Oxford move-

ment, was intrusted to my friend Mr. Frederick Faber. I told
him what I wished to be said, and begged that, as he was inti-
mately acquainted with several of the Leaders of it, he would
express my thought in the way least likely to be taken amiss by
them. Much of the work they are undertaking was grievously
wanted, and God grant their endeavours may continue to pros-
per as they have done.

YE Apennines! with all your fertile vales
Deeply embosomed, and your winding shores
Of either sea — an Islander by birth,
A Mountaineer by habit, would resound
Your praise, in meet accordance with your claims
Bestowed by Nature, or from man's great deeds
Inherited: — presumptuous thought! — it fled
Like vapour, like a towering cloud, dissolved.
Not, therefore, shall my mind give way to sadness; —
Yon snow-white torrent-fall, plumb down it drops
Yet ever hangs or seems to hang in air,
Lulling the leisure of that high perched town,
AQUAPENDENTE, in her lofty site
Its neighbour and its namesake — town, and flood
Forth flashing out of its own gloomy chasm
Bright sunbeams — the fresh verdure of this lawn
Strewn with grey rocks, and on the horizon's verge,
O'er intervenient waste, through glimmering haze,
Unquestionably kenned, that cone-shaped hill
With fractured summit, no indifferent sight

To travellers, from such comforts as are thine,
Bleak Radicofani! escaped with joy —
These are before me; and the varied scene
May well suffice, till noon-tide's sultry heat
Relax, to fix and satisfy the mind
Passive yet pleased. What! with this Broom in flower
Close at my side! She bids me fly to greet
Her sisters, soon like her to be attired
With golden blossoms opening at the feet
Of my own Fairfield. The glad greeting given,
Given with a voice and by a look returned
Of old companionship, Time counts not minutes
Ere, from accustomed paths, familiar fields,
The local Genius hurries me aloft,
Transported over that cloud-wooing hill,
Seat Sandal, a fond suitor of the clouds,
With dream-like smoothness, to Helvellyn's top,
There to alight upon crisp moss and range,
Obtaining ampler boon, at every step,
Of visual sovereignty — hills multitudinous,
(Not Apennine can boast of fairer) hills
Pride of two nations, wood and lake and plains,
And prospect right below of deep coves shaped
By skeleton arms, that, from the mountain's trunk
Extended, clasp the winds, with mutual moan
Struggling for liberty, while undismayed

MUSINGS NEAR AQUAPENDENTE

The shepherd struggles with them. Onward thence
And downward by the skirt of Greenside fell,
And by Glenridding-screes, and low Glencoign,
Places forsaken now, though loving still
The muses, as they loved them in the days
Of the old minstrels and the border bards. —
But here am I fast bound; and let it pass,
The simple rapture; — who that travels far
To feed his mind with watchful eyes could share
Or wish to share it? — One there surely was,
"The Wizard of the North," with anxious hope
Brought to this genial climate, when disease
Preyed upon body and mind — yet not the less
Had his sunk eye kindled at those dear words
That spake of bards and minstrels; and his spirit
Had flown with mine to old Helvellyn's brow,
Where once together, in his day of strength,
We stood rejoicing, as if earth were free
From sorrow, like the sky above our heads.
     Years followed years, and when, upon the eve
Of his last going from Tweed-side, thought turned,
Or by another's sympathy was led,
To this bright land, Hope was for him no friend,
Knowledge no help; Imagination shaped
No promise. Still, in more than ear-deep seats,
Survives for me, and cannot but survive

The tone of voice which wedded borrowed words
To sadness not their own, when, with faint smile
Forced by intent to take from speech its edge,
He said, "When I am there, although 't is fair,
'T will be another Yarrow." [6] Prophecy
More than fulfilled, as gay Campania's shores
Soon witnessed, and the city of seven hills,
Her sparkling fountains and her mouldering tombs;
And more than all, that Eminence which showed
Her splendours, seen, not felt, the while he stood
A few short steps (painful they were) apart
From Tasso's Convent-haven, and retired grave.

    Peace to their Spirits! why should Poesy
Yield to the lure of vain regret, and hover
In gloom on wings with confidence outspread
To move in sunshine? — Utter thanks, my Soul!
Tempered with awe, and sweetened by compassion
For them who in the shades of sorrow dwell,
That I — so near the term to human life
Appointed by man's common heritage,
Frail as the frailest, one withal (if that
Deserve a thought) but little known to fame —
Am free to rove where Nature's loveliest looks,
Art's noblest relics, history's rich bequests,
Failed to reanimate and but feebly cheered
The whole world's Darling — free to rove at will

O'er high and low, and if requiring rest,
  Rest from enjoyment only.
                  Thanks poured forth
For what thus far hath blessed my wanderings, thanks
Fervent but humble as the lips can breathe
Where gladness seems a duty — let me guard
Those seeds of expectation which the fruit
Already gathered in this favoured Land
Enfolds within its core. The faith be mine,
That He who guides and governs all, approves
When gratitude, though disciplined to look
Beyond these transient spheres, doth wear a crown
Of earthly hope put on with trembling hand;
Nor is least pleased, we trust, when golden beams,
Reflected through the mists of age, from hours
Of innocent delight, remote or recent,
Shoot but a little way — 't is all they can —
Into the doubtful future. Who would keep
Power must resolve to cleave to it through life,
Else it deserts him, surely as he lives.
Saints would not grieve nor guardian angels frown
If one — while tossed, as was my lot to be,
In a frail bark urged by two slender oars
Over waves rough and deep, that, when they broke,
Dashed their white foam against the palace walls
Of Genoa the superb — should there be led

To meditate upon his own appointed tasks,
However humble in themselves, with thoughts
Raised and sustained by memory of Him
Who oftentimes within those narrow bounds
Rocked on the surge, there tried his spirit's strength
And grasp of purpose, long ere sailed his ship
To lay a new world open.

               Nor less prized
Be those impressions which incline the heart
To mild, to lowly, and to seeming weak,
Bend that way her desires. The dew, the storm —
The dew whose moisture fell in gentle drops
On the small hyssop destined to become,
By Hebrew ordinance devoutly kept,
A purifying instrument — the storm
That shook on Lebanon the cedar's top,
And as it shook, enabling the blind roots
Further to force their way, endowed its trunk
With magnitude and strength fit to uphold
The glorious temple — did alike proceed
From the same gracious will, were both an offspring
Of bounty infinite.

            Between Powers that aim
Higher to lift their lofty heads, impelled
By no profane ambition, Powers that thrive
By conflict, and their opposites, that trust

MUSINGS NEAR AQUAPENDENTE

In lowliness — a midway tract there lies
Of thoughtful sentiment for every mind
Pregnant with good. Young, Middle-aged, and Old,
From century on to century, must have known
The emotion — nay, more fitly were it said —
The blest tranquillity that sunk so deep
Into my spirit, when I paced, enclosed
In Pisa's Campo Santo, the smooth floor
Of its Arcades paved with sepulchral slabs,
And through each window's open fretwork looked
O'er the blank Area of sacred earth
Fetched from Mount Calvary, or haply delved
In precincts nearer to the Saviour's tomb,
By hands of men, humble as brave, who fought
For its deliverance — a capacious field
That to descendants of the dead it holds
And to all living mute memento breathes,
More touching far than aught which on the walls
Is pictured, or their epitaphs can speak,
Of the changed City's long-departed power,
Glory, and wealth, which, perilous as they are,
Here did not kill, but nourished, Piety.
And, high above that length of cloistral roof,
Peering in air and backed by azure sky,
To kindred contemplations ministers
The Baptistery's dome, and that which swells

[73]

From the Cathedral pile; and with the twain
Conjoined in prospect mutable or fixed
(As hurry on in eagerness the feet,
Or pause) the summit of the Leaning-tower.
Nor less remuneration waits on him
Who having left the Cemetery stands
In the Tower's shadow, of decline and fall
Admonished not without some sense of fear,
Fear that soon vanishes before the sight
Of splendour unextinguished, pomp unscathed,
And beauty unimpaired. Grand in itself,
And for itself, the assemblage, grand and fair
To view, and for the mind's consenting eye
A type of age in man, upon its front
Bearing the world-acknowledged evidence
Of past exploits, nor fondly after more
Struggling against the stream of destiny,
But with its peaceful majesty content.
— Oh what a spectacle at every turn
The Place unfolds, from pavement skinned with moss
Or grass-grown spaces, where the heaviest foot
Provokes no echoes, but must softly tread;
Where Solitude with Silence paired stops short
Of Desolation, and to Ruin's scythe
Decay submits not.
                                    But where'er my steps

[74]

MUSINGS NEAR AQUAPENDENTE

Shall wander, chiefly let me cull with care
Those images of genial beauty, oft
Too lovely to be pensive in themselves
But by reflection made so, which do best
And fitliest serve to crown with fragrant wreaths
Life's cup when almost filled with years, like mine.
— How lovely robed in forenoon light and shade,
Each ministering to each, didst thou appear
Savona, Queen of territory fair
As aught that marvellous coast thro' all its length
Yields to the Stranger's eye. Remembrance holds
As a selected treasure thy one cliff,
That, while it wore for melancholy crest
A shattered Convent, yet rose proud to have
Clinging to its steep sides a thousand herbs
And shrubs, whose pleasant looks gave proof how kind
The breath of air can be where earth had else
Seemed churlish. And behold, both far and near,
Garden and field all decked with orange bloom,
And peach and citron, in Spring's mildest breeze
Expanding; and, along the smooth shore curved
Into a natural port, a tideless sea,
To that mild breeze with motion and with voice
Softly responsive; and, attuned to all
Those vernal charms of sight and sound, appeared
Smooth space of turf which from the guardian fort

Sloped seaward, turf whose tender April green,
In coolest climes too fugitive, might even here
Plead with the sovereign Sun for longer stay
Than his unmitigated beams allow,
Nor plead in vain, if beauty could preserve,
From mortal change, aught that is born on earth
Or doth on time depend.
                    While on the brink
Of that high Convent-crested cliff I stood,
Modest Savona! over all did brood
A pure poetic Spirit — as the breeze,
Mild — as the verdure, fresh — the sunshine, bright—
Thy gentle Chiabrera! — not a stone,
Mural or level with the trodden floor,
In Church or Chapel, if my curious quest
Missed not the truth, retains a single name
Of young or old, warrior, or saint, or sage,
To whose dear memories his sepulchral verse[7]
Paid simple tribute, such as might have flowed
From the clear spring of a plain English heart,
Say rather, one in native fellowship
With all who want not skill to couple grief
With praise, as genuine admiration prompts.
The grief, the praise, are severed from their dust,
Yet in his page the records of that worth
Survive, uninjured; — glory then to words,

MUSINGS NEAR AQUAPENDENTE

Honour to word-preserving Arts, and hail
Ye kindred local influences that still,
If Hope's familiar whispers merit faith,
Await my steps when they the breezy height
Shall range of philosophic Tusculum;
Or Sabine vales explored inspire a wish
To meet the shade of Horace by the side
Of his Bandusian fount; or I invoke
His presence to point out the spot where once
He sate, and eulogized with earnest pen
Peace, leisure, freedom, moderate desires;
And all the immunities of rural life
Extolled, behind Vacuna's crumbling fane.
Or let me loiter, soothed with what is given
Nor asking more, on that delicious Bay,
Parthenope's Domain — Virgilian haunt,
Illustrated with never-dying verse,
And, by the Poet's laurel-shaded tomb,
Age after age to Pilgrims from all lands
Endeared.
　　　　　And who — if not a man as cold
In heart as dull in brain — while pacing ground
Chosen by Rome's legendary Bards, high minds
Out of her early struggles well inspired
To localize heroic acts — could look
Upon the spots with undelighted eye,

Though even to their last syllable the Lays
And very names of those who gave them birth
Have perished? — Verily, to her utmost depth,
Imagination feels what Reason fears not
To recognize, the lasting virtue lodged
In those bold fictions that, by deeds assigned
To the Valerian, Fabian, Curian Race,
And others like in fame, created Powers
With attributes from History derived,
By Poesy irradiate, and yet graced,
Through marvellous felicity of skill,
With something more propitious to high aims
Than either, pent within her separate sphere,
Can oft with justice claim.
                               And not disdaining
Union with those primeval energies
To virtue consecrate, stoop ye from your height
Christian Traditions! at my Spirit's call
Descend, and, on the brow of ancient Rome
As she survives in ruin, manifest
Your glories mingled with the brightest hues
Of her memorial halo, fading, fading,
But never to be extinct while Earth endures.
O come, if undishonoured by the prayer,
From all her Sanctuaries! — Open for my feet
Ye Catacombs, give to mine eyes a glimpse

Of the Devout, as, 'mid your glooms convened
For safety, they of yore enclasped the Cross
On knees that ceased from trembling, or intoned
Their orisons with voices half-suppressed,
But sometimes heard, or fancied to be heard,
Even at this hour.

        And thou Mamertine prison,
Into that vault receive me from whose depth
Issues, revealed in no presumptuous vision,
Albeit lifting human to divine,
A Saint, the Church's Rock, the mystic Keys
Grasped in his hand; and lo! with upright sword
Prefiguring his own impendent doom,
The Apostle of the Gentiles; both prepared
To suffer pains with heathen scorn and hate
Inflicted; — blessèd Men, for so to Heaven
They follow their dear Lord!

        Time flows — nor winds,
Nor stagnates, nor precipitates his course,
But many a benefit borne upon his breast
For human-kind sinks out of sight, is gone,
No one knows how; nor seldom is put forth
An angry arm that snatches good away,
Never perhaps to reappear. The Stream
Has to our generation brought and brings
Innumerable gains; yet we, who now

Walk in the light of day, pertain full surely
To a chilled age, most pitiably shut out
From that which *is* and actuates, by forms,
Abstractions, and by lifeless fact to fact
Minutely linked with diligence uninspired,
Unrectified, unguided, unsustained,
By godlike insight. To this fate is doomed
Science, wide-spread and spreading still as be
Her conquests, in the world of sense made known,
So with the internal mind it fares; and so
With morals, trusting, in contempt or fear
Of vital principle's controlling law,
To her purblind guide Expediency; and so
Suffers religious faith. Elate with view
Of what is won, we overlook or scorn
The best that should keep pace with it, and must,
Else more and more the general mind will droop,
Even as if bent on perishing. There lives
No faculty within us which the Soul
Can spare, and humblest earthly Weal demands,
For dignity not placed beyond her reach,
Zealous co-operation of all means
Given or acquired, to raise us from the mire,
And liberate our hearts from low pursuits.
By gross Utilities enslaved, we need
More of ennobling impulse from the past,

If to the future aught of good must come
Sounder and therefore holier than the ends
Which, in the giddiness of self-applause,
We covet as supreme. O grant the crown
That Wisdom wears, or take his treacherous staff
From Knowledge! — If the Muse, whom I have
    served
This day, be mistress of a single pearl
Fit to be placed in that pure diadem;
Then, not in vain, under these chestnut boughs
Reclined, shall I have yielded up my soul
To transports from the secondary founts
Flowing of time and place, and paid to both
Due homage; nor shall fruitlessly have striven,
By love of beauty moved, to enshrine in verse
Accordant meditations, which in times
Vexed and disordered, as our own, may shed
Influence, at least among a scattered few,
To soberness of mind and peace of heart
Friendly; as here to my repose hath been
This flowering broom's dear neighbourhood, the
    light
And murmur issuing from yon pendent flood,
And all the varied landscape. Let us now
Rise, and to-morrow greet magnificent Rome.[8]

[81]

II

THE PINE OF MONTE MARIO AT ROME

1837 1842

Sir George Beaumont told me that, when he first visited Italy, pine-trees of this species abounded, but that on his return thither, which was more than thirty years after, they had disappeared from many places where he had been accustomed to admire them, and had become rare all over the country, especially in and about Rome. Several Roman villas have within these few years passed into the hands of foreigners, who, I observed with pleasure, have taken care to plant this tree, which in course of years will become a great ornament to the city and to the general landscape. May I venture to add here, that having ascended the Monte Mario, I could not resist embracing the trunk of this interesting monument of my departed friend's feelings for the beauties of nature, and the power of that art which he loved so much, and in the practice of which he was so distinguished.

I saw far off the dark top of a Pine
Look like a cloud — a slender stem the tie
That bound it to its native earth — poised high,
'Mid evening hues, along the horizon line,
Striving in peace each other to outshine.
But when I learned the Tree was living there,
Saved from the sordid axe by Beaumont's care,[9]
Oh, what a gush of tenderness was mine!

[82]

THE PINE OF MONTE MARIO

The rescued Pine-Tree, with its sky so bright
And cloud-like beauty, rich in thoughts of home,
Death-parted friends, and days too swift in flight,
Supplanted the whole majesty of Rome
(Then first apparent from the Pincian Height)
Crowned with St. Peter's everlasting Dome.

III

AT ROME

1837   1842

Sight is at first a sad enemy to imagination and to those
pleasures belonging to old times with which some exertions of
that power will always mingle: nothing perhaps brings this
truth home to the feelings more than the city of Rome; not so
much in respect to the impression made at the moment when it
is first seen and looked at as a whole, for then the imagination
may be invigorated and the mind's eye quickened; but when
particular spots or objects are sought out, disappointment is I
believe invariably felt. Ability to recover from this disappoint-
ment will exist in proportion to knowledge, and the power of
the mind to reconstruct out of fragments and parts, and to
make details in the present subservient to more adequate com-
prehension of the past.

Is this, ye Gods, the Capitolian Hill?
Yon petty Steep in truth the fearful Rock,
Tarpeian named of yore, and keeping still
That name, a local Phantom proud to mock
The Traveller's expectation? — Could our Will
Destroy the ideal Power within, 't were done
Thro' what men see and touch, — slaves wandering
    on,
Impelled by thirst of all but Heaven-taught skill.
Full oft, our wish obtained, deeply we sigh;

AT ROME

Yet not unrecompensed are they who learn,
From that depression raised, to mount on high
With stronger wing, more clearly to discern
Eternal things; and, if need be, defy
Change, with a brow not insolent, though stern.

IV

AT ROME — REGRETS — IN ALLUSION TO NIEBUHR AND OTHER MODERN HISTORIANS

1837   1842

THOSE old credulities, to nature dear,
Shall they no longer bloom upon the stock
Of History, stript naked as a rock
'Mid a dry desert? What is it we hear?
The glory of Infant Rome must disappear,
Her morning splendours vanish, and their place
Know them no more. If Truth, who veiled her face
With those bright beams yet hid it not, must steer
Henceforth a humbler course perplexed and slow;
One solace yet remains for us who came
Into this world in days when story lacked
Severe research, that in our hearts we know
How, for exciting youth's heroic flame,
Assent is power, belief the soul of fact.[10]

V

CONTINUED

1837–42   1842

COMPLACENT Fictions were they, yet the same
Involved a history of no doubtful sense,
History that proves by inward evidence
From what a precious source of truth it came.
Ne'er could the boldest Eulogist have dared
Such deeds to paint, such characters to frame,
But for coeval sympathy prepared
To greet with instant faith their loftiest claim.
None but a noble people could have loved
Flattery in Ancient Rome's pure-minded style:
Not in like sort the Runic Scald was moved;
He, nursed 'mid savage passions that defile
Humanity, sang feats that well might call
For the blood-thirsty mead of Odin's riotous Hall.

VI

PLEA FOR THE HISTORIAN

1837-42   1842

FORBEAR to deem the Chronicler unwise,
Ungentle, or untouched by seemly ruth,
Who, gathering up all that Time's envious tooth
Has spared of sound and grave realities,
Firmly rejects those dazzling flatteries,
Dear as they are to unsuspecting Youth,
That might have drawn down Clio from the skies
To vindicate the majesty of truth.
Such was her office while she walked with men,
A Muse, who, not unmindful of her Sire
All-ruling Jove, whate'er the theme might be,
Revered her Mother, sage Mnemosyne,
And taught her faithful servants how the lyre
Should animate, but not mislead, the pen.[10]

VII

AT ROME

1837-42 1842

I have a private interest in this Sonnet, for I doubt whether it would ever have been written but for the lively picture given me by Anna Ricketts of what they had witnessed of the indignation and sorrow expressed by some Italian noblemen of their acquaintance upon the surrender, which circumstances had obliged them to make, of the best portion of their family mansions to strangers.

THEY — who have seen the noble Roman's scorn
Break forth at thought of laying down his head,
When the blank day is over, garreted
In his ancestral palace, where, from morn
To night, the desecrated floors are worn
By feet of purse-proud strangers; they — who have read
In one meek smile, beneath a peasant's shed,
How patiently the weight of wrong is borne;
They — who have heard some learned Patriot treat
Of freedom, with mind grasping the whole theme
From ancient Rome, downwards through that bright
      dream
Of Commonwealths, each city a starlike seat
Of rival glory; they — fallen Italy —
Nor must, nor will, nor can, despair of Thee!

[89]

VIII

NEAR ROME, IN SIGHT OF ST. PETER'S

1837–42 1842

Long has the dew been dried on tree and lawn:
O'er man and beast a not unwelcome boon
Is shed, the languor of approaching noon;
To shady rest withdrawing or withdrawn
Mute are all creatures, as this couchant fawn,
Save insect-swarms that hum in air afloat,
Save that the Cock is crowing, a shrill note,
Startling and shrill as that which roused the dawn.
— Heard in that hour, or when, as now, the nerve
Shrinks from the note as from a mistimed thing,
Oft for a holy warning may it serve,
Charged with remembrance of *his* sudden sting,
His bitter tears, whose name the Papal Chair
And yon resplendent Church are proud to bear.

IX

AT ALBANO

1837-42 1842

This Sonnet is founded on simple fact, and was written to enlarge, if possible, the views of those who can see nothing but evil in the intercessions countenanced by the Church of Rome. That they are in many respects lamentably pernicious must be acknowledged; but, on the other hand, they who reflect, while they see and observe, cannot but be struck with instances which will prove that it is a great error to condemn in all cases such mediation as purely idolatrous. This remark bears with especial force upon addresses to the Virgin.

DAYS passed — and Monte Calvo would not clear
His head from mist; and, as the wind sobbed through
Albano's dripping Ilex avenue,
My dull forebodings in a Peasant's ear
Found casual vent. She said, "Be of good cheer;
Our yesterday's procession did not sue
In vain; the sky will change to sunny blue,
Thanks to our Lady's grace." I smiled to hear,
But not in scorn: — the Matron's Faith may lack
The heavenly sanction needed to ensure
Fulfilment; but, we trust, her upward track
Stops not at this low point, nor wants the lure
Of flowers the Virgin without fear may own,
For by her Son's blest hand the seed was sown.

[91]

X

1837–42   1842

NEAR Anio's stream, I spied a gentle Dove
Perched on an olive branch, and heard her cooing
'Mid new-born blossoms that soft airs were wooing,
While all things present told of joy and love.
But restless Fancy left that olive grove
To hail the exploratory Bird renewing
Hope for the few, who, at the world's undoing,
On the great flood were spared to live and move.
O bounteous Heaven! signs true as dove and bough
Brought to the ark are coming evermore,
Given though we seek them not, but, while we plough
This sea of life without a visible shore,
Do neither promise ask nor grace implore
In what alone is ours, the living Now.

XI

FROM THE ALBAN HILLS, LOOKING TOWARDS ROME

1837–42 1842

FORGIVE, illustrious Country! these deep sighs,
Heaved less for thy bright plains and hills bestrown
With monuments decayed or overthrown,
For all that tottering stands or prostrate lies,
Than for like scenes in moral vision shown,
Ruin perceived for keener sympathies;
Faith crushed, yet proud of weeds, her gaudy crown;
Virtues laid low, and mouldering energies.
Yet why prolong this mournful strain? — Fallen
    Power,
Thy fortunes, twice exalted, might provoke
Verse to glad notes prophetic of the hour
When thou, uprisen, shalt break thy double yoke,
And enter, with prompt aid from the Most High,
On the third stage of thy great destiny.

XII

NEAR THE LAKE OF THRASYMENE

1837–42 1842

WHEN here with Carthage Rome to conflict came,
An earthquake, mingling with the battle's shock,
Checked not its rage; unfelt the ground did rock,
Sword dropped not, javelin kept its deadly aim. —
Now all is sun-bright peace. Of that day's shame,
Or glory, not a vestige seems to endure,
Save in this Rill[11] that took from blood the name
Which yet it bears, sweet Stream! as crystal pure.
So may all trace and sign of deeds aloof
From the true guidance of humanity,
Thro' Time and Nature's influence, purify
Their spirit; or, unless they for reproof
Or warning serve, thus let them all, on ground
That gave them being, vanish to a sound.

XIII

NEAR THE SAME LAKE

1837–42 1842

FOR action born, existing to be tried,
Powers manifold we have that intervene
To stir the heart that would too closely screen
Her peace from images to pain allied.
What wonder if at midnight, by the side
Of Sanguinetto, or broad Thrasymene,
The clang of arms is heard, and phantoms glide,
Unhappy ghosts in troops by moonlight seen;
And singly thine, O vanquished Chief! whose corse,
Unburied, lay hid under heaps of slain:
But who is He? — the Conqueror. Would he force
His way to Rome? Ah, no, — round hill and plain
Wandering, he haunts, at fancy's strong command,
This spot — his shadowy death-cup in his hand.

XIV

THE CUCKOO AT LAVERNA

MAY 25, 1837

1837   1842

Among a thousand delightful feelings connected in my mind
with the voice of the cuckoo, there is a personal one which is
rather melancholy. I was first convinced that age had rather
dulled my hearing, by not being able to catch the sound at the
same distance as the younger companions of my walks; and of
this failure I had a proof upon the occasion that suggested
these verses. I did not hear the sound till Mr. Robinson had
twice or thrice directed my attention to it.

LIST — 't was the Cuckoo. — O with what delight
Heard I that voice! and catch it now, though faint,
Far off and faint, and melting into air,
Yet not to be mistaken. Hark again!
Those louder cries give notice that the Bird,
Although invisible as Echo's self,
Is wheeling hitherward. Thanks, happy Creature,
For this unthought-of greeting!
                                    While allured
From vale to hill, from hill to vale led on,
We have pursued, through various lands, a long
And pleasant course; flower after flower has blown,

THE CUCKOO AT LAVERNA

Embellishing the ground that gave them birth
With aspects novel to my sight; but still
Most fair, most welcome, when they drank the dew
In a sweet fellowship with kinds beloved,
For old remembrance sake. And oft — where Spring
Displayed her richest blossoms among files
Of orange-trees bedecked with glowing fruit
Ripe for the hand, or under a thick shade
Of Ilex, or, if better suited to the hour,
The lightsome Olive's twinkling canopy —
Oft have I heard the Nightingale and Thrush
Blending as in a common English grove
Their love-songs; but, where'er my feet might roam,
Whate'er assemblages of new and old,
Strange and familiar, might beguile the way,
A gratulation from that vagrant Voice
Was wanting, — and most happily till now.

For see, Laverna! mark the far-famed Pile,
High on the brink of that precipitous rock,
Implanted like a Fortress, as in truth
It is, a Christian Fortress, garrisoned
In faith and hope, and dutiful obedience,
By a few Monks, a stern society,
Dead to the world and scorning earth-born joys.
Nay—though the hopes that drew, the fears that drove,
St. Francis, far from Man's resort, to abide

Among these sterile heights of Apennine,
Bound him, nor, since he raised yon House, have ceased
To bind his spiritual Progeny, with rules
Stringent as flesh can tolerate and live;
His milder Genius (thanks to the good God
That made us) over those severe restraints
Of mind, that dread heart-freezing discipline,
Doth sometimes here predominate, and works
By unsought means for gracious purposes;
For earth through heaven, for heaven, by changeful
    earth,
Illustrated, and mutually endeared.

  Rapt though He were above the power of sense,
Familiarly, yet out of the cleansed heart
Of that once sinful Being overflowed
On sun, moon, stars, the nether elements,
And every shape of creature they sustain,
Divine affections; and with beast and bird
(Stilled from afar — such marvel story tells —
By casual outbreak of his passionate words,
And from their own pursuits in field or grove
Drawn to his side by look or act of love
Humane, and virtue of his innocent life)
He wont to hold companionship so free,
So pure, so fraught with knowledge and delight,
As to be likened in his Followers' minds

THE CUCKOO AT LAVERNA

To that which our first Parents, ere the fall
From their high state darkened the Earth with fear,
Held with all kinds in Eden's blissful bowers.

  Then question not that, 'mid the austere Band,
Who breathe the air he breathed, tread where he trod,
Some true Partakers of his loving spirit
Do still survive, and, with those gentle hearts
Consorted, Others, in the power, the faith,
Of a baptized imagination, prompt
To catch from Nature's humblest monitors
Whate'er they bring of impulses sublime.

  Thus sensitive must be the Monk, though pale
With fasts, with vigils worn, depressed by years,
Whom in a sunny glade I chanced to see,
Upon a pine-tree's storm-uprooted trunk,
Seated alone, with forehead sky-ward raised,
Hands clasped above the crucifix he wore
Appended to his bosom, and lips closed
By the joint pressure of his musing mood
And habit of his vow. That ancient Man —
Nor haply less the Brother whom I marked,
As we approached the Convent gate, aloft
Looking far forth from his aërial cell,
A young Ascetic — Poet, Hero, Sage,
He might have been, Lover belike he was —
If they received into a conscious ear

The notes whose first faint greeting startled me,
Whose sedulous iteration thrilled with joy
My heart — may have been moved like me to think,
Ah! not like me who walk in the world's ways,
On the great Prophet, styled *the Voice of One
Crying amid the wilderness*, and given,
Now that their snows must melt, their herbs and
      flowers
Revive, their obstinate winter pass away,
That awful name to Thee, thee, simple Cuckoo,
Wandering in solitude, and evermore
Foretelling and proclaiming, ere thou leave
This thy last haunt beneath Italian skies
To carry thy glad tidings over heights
Still loftier, and to climes more near the Pole.

    Voice of the Desert, fare-thee-well; sweet Bird!
If that substantial title please thee more,
Farewell! — but go thy way, no need hast thou
Of a good wish sent after thee; from bower
To bower as green, from sky to sky as clear,
Thee gentle breezes waft — or airs, that meet
Thy course and sport around thee, softly fan —
Till Night, descending upon hill and vale,
Grants to thy mission a brief term of silence,
And folds thy pinions up in blest repose.

[100]

XV

AT THE CONVENT OF CAMALDOLI[12]

1837-42 1842

GRIEVE for the Man who hither came bereft,
And seeking consolation from above;
Nor grieve the less that skill to him was left
To paint this picture of his lady-love:
Can she, a blessed saint, the work approve?
And oh, good Brethren of the cowl, a thing
So fair, to which with peril he must cling,
Destroy in pity, or with care remove.
That bloom — those eyes — can they assist to bind
Thoughts that would stray from Heaven? The dream
        must cease
To be; by Faith, not sight, his soul must live;
Else will the enamoured Monk too surely find
How wide a space can part from inward peace
The most profound repose his cell can give.

XVI

CONTINUED

1837–42   1842

THE world forsaken, all its busy cares
And stirring interests shunned with desperate flight,
All trust abandoned in the healing might
Of virtuous action; all that courage dares,
Labour accomplishes, or patience bears —
Those helps rejected, they, whose minds perceive
How subtly works man's weakness, sighs may heave
For such a One beset with clöistral snares.
Father of Mercy! rectify his view,
If with his vows this object ill agree;
Shed over it thy grace, and thus subdue
Imperious passion in a heart set free: —
That earthly love may to herself be true,
Give him a soul that cleaveth unto thee.

XVII

AT THE EREMITE OR UPPER CONVENT
OF CAMALDOLI

1837–42 1842

WHAT aim had they, the Pair of Monks,[13] in size
Enormous, dragged, while side by side they sate,
By panting steers up to this convent gate?
How, with empurpled cheeks and pampered eyes,
Dare they confront the lean austerities
Of Brethren who, here fixed, on Jesu wait
In sackcloth, and God's anger deprecate
Through all that humbles flesh and mortifies?
Strange contrast! — verily the world of dreams,
Where mingle, as for mockery combined,
Things in their very essences at strife,
Shows not a sight incongruous as the extremes
That everywhere, before the thoughtful mind,
Meet on the solid ground of waking life.

XVIII

AT VALLOMBROSA[14]

1837–42   1842

"Thick as autumnal leaves that strew the brooks
In Vallombrosa, where Etrurian shades
High over-arch'd embower."   *Paradise Lost.*

I must confess, though of course I did not acknowledge it in
the few lines I wrote in the Strangers' book kept at the con-
vent, that I was somewhat disappointed at Vallombrosa. I
had expected, as the name implies, a deep and narrow valley
overshadowed by enclosing hills; but the spot where the con-
vent stands is in fact not a valley at all, but a cove or cres-
cent open to an extensive prospect. In the book before men-
tioned, I read the notice in the English language that if any one
would ascend the steep ground above the convent, and wander
over it, he would be abundantly rewarded by magnificent
views. I had not time to act upon this recommendation, and
only went with my young guide to a point, nearly on a level
with the site of the convent, that overlooks the vale of Arno
for some leagues. To praise great and good men has ever been
deemed one of the worthiest employments of poetry, but the
objects of admiration vary so much with time and circum-
stances, and the noblest of mankind have been found, when
intimately known, to be of characters so imperfect, that no
eulogist can find a subject which he will venture upon with the
animation necessary to create sympathy, unless he confines
himself to a particular art or he takes something of a one-sided
view of the person he is disposed to celebrate. This is a melan-
choly truth, and affords a strong reason for the poetic mind

being chiefly exercised in works of fiction: the poet can then
follow wherever the spirit of admiration leads him, unchecked
by such suggestions as will be too apt to cross his way if all
that he is prompted to utter is to be tested by fact. Something
in this spirit I have written in the note attached to the sonnet
on the king of Sweden; and many will think that in this poem
and elsewhere I have spoken of the author of "Paradise Lost"
in a strain of panegyric scarcely justifiable by the tenor of
some of his opinions, whether theological or political, and by
the temper he carried into public affairs in which, unfortun-
ately for his genius, he was so much concerned.

"Vallombrosa — I longed in thy shadiest wood
To slumber, reclined on the moss-covered floor!"[15]
Fond wish that was granted at last, and the Flood,
That lulled me asleep bids me listen once more.
Its murmur how soft! as it falls down the steep,
Near that Cell — yon sequestered Retreat high in
    air —
Where our Milton was wont lonely vigils to keep
For converse with God, sought through study and
    prayer.
The Monks still repeat the tradition with pride,
And its truth who shall doubt? for his Spirit is here;
In the cloud-piercing rocks doth her grandeur abide,
In the pines pointing heavenward her beauty austere;
In the flower-besprent meadows his genius we trace
Turned to humbler delights, in which youth might con-
    fide,

That would yield him fit help while prefiguring that
    Place
Where, if Sin had not entered, Love never had died.

When with life lengthened out came a desolate time,
And darkness and danger had compassed him round,
With a thought he would flee to these haunts of his
    prime
And here once again a kind shelter be found.
And let me believe that when nightly the Muse
Did waft him to Sion, the glorified hill,
Here also, on some favoured height, he would choose
To wander, and drink inspiration at will.

Vallombrosa! of thee I first heard in the page
Of that holiest of Bards, and the name for my mind
Had a musical charm, which the winter of age
And the changes it brings had no power to unbind.
And now, ye Miltonian shades! under you
I repose, nor am forced from sweet fancy to part,
While your leaves I behold and the brooks they will
    strew,
And the realised vision is clasped to my heart.

Even so, and unblamed, we rejoice as we may
In Forms that must perish, frail objects of sense;

AT VALLOMBROSA

Unblamed — if the Soul be intent on the day
When the Being of Beings shall summon her hence.
For he and he only with wisdom is blest
Who, gathering true pleasures wherever they grow,
Looks up in all places, for joy or for rest,
To the Fountain whence Time and Eternity flow.

XIX

AT FLORENCE

1837–42 1842

Upon what evidence the belief rests that this stone was a favourite seat of Dante, I do not know; but a man would little consult his own interest as a traveller, if he should busy himself with doubts as to the fact. The readiness with which traditions of this character are received, and the fidelity with which they are preserved from generation to generation, are an evidence of feelings honourable to our nature. I remember how, during one of my rambles in the course of a college vacation, I was pleased on being shown a seat near a kind of rocky cell at the source of the river, on which it was said that Congreve wrote his "Old Bachelor." One can scarcely hit on any performance less in harmony with the scene; but it was a local tribute paid to intellect by those who had not troubled themselves to estimate the moral worth of that author's comedies; and why should they? He was a man distinguished in his day; and the sequestered neighbourhood in which he often resided was perhaps as proud of him as Florence of her Dante: it is the same feeling, though proceeding from persons one cannot bring together in this way without offering some apology to the Shade of the great Visionary.

UNDER the shadow of a stately Pile,
The dome of Florence, pensive and alone,
Nor giving heed to aught that passed the while,
I stood, and gazed upon a marble stone,

[108]

AT FLORENCE

The laurelled Dante's favourite seat. A throne,
In just esteem, it rivals; though no style
Be there of decoration to beguile
The mind, depressed by thought of greatness flown.
As a true man, who long had served the lyre,
I gazed with earnestness, and dared no more.
But in his breast the mighty Poet bore
A Patriot's heart, warm with undying fire.
Bold with the thought, in reverence I sate down,
And, for a moment, filled that empty Throne.

XX

BEFORE THE PICTURE OF THE BAPTIST, BY RAPHAEL, IN THE GALLERY AT FLORENCE

1837–42 1842

It was very hot weather during the week we stayed at Florence; and, never having been there before, I went through much hard service, and am not therefore *ashamed* to confess I fell asleep before this picture and sitting with my back towards the Venus de Médicis. Buonaparte — in answer to one who had spoken of his being in a sound sleep up to the moment when one of his great battles was to be fought, as a proof of the calmness of his mind and command over anxious thoughts — said frankly, that he slept because from bodily exhaustion he could not help it. In like manner it is noticed that criminals on the night previous to their execution seldom awake before they are called, a proof that the body is the master of us far more than we need be willing to allow. Should this note by any possible chance be seen by any of my countrymen who might have been in the gallery at the time (and several persons were there) and witnessed such an indecorum, I hope he will give up the opinion which he might naturally have formed to my prejudice.

THE Baptist might have been ordained to cry
Forth from the towers of that huge Pile, wherein
His Father served Jehovah; but how win
Due audience, how for aught but scorn defy

[110]

RAPHAEL'S JOHN THE BAPTIST

The obstinate pride and wanton revelry
Of the Jerusalem below, her sin
And folly, if they with united din
Drown not at once mandate and prophecy?
Therefore the Voice spake from the Desert, thence
To Her, as to her opposite in peace,
Silence, and holiness, and innocence,
To Her and to all Lands its warning sent,
Crying with earnestness that might not cease,
"Make straight a highway for the Lord — repent!"

XXI

AT FLORENCE — FROM MICHAEL ANGELO

1837–42   1842

However at first these two sonnets from Michael Angelo
may seem in their spirit somewhat inconsistent with each
other, I have not scrupled to place them side by side as char-
acteristic of their great author, and others with whom he lived.
I feel nevertheless a wish to know at what periods of his life
they were respectively composed. The latter, as it expresses,
was written in his advanced years when it was natural that
the Platonism that pervades the one should give way to the
Christian feeling that inspired the other: between both there
is more than poetic affinity.

RAPT above earth by power of one fair face,
Hers in whose sway alone my heart delights,
I mingle with the blest on those pure heights
Where Man, yet mortal, rarely finds a place.
With Him who made the Work that Work accords
So well, that by its help and through his grace
I raise my thoughts, inform my deeds and words,
Clasping her beauty in my soul's embrace.
Thus, if from two fair eyes mine cannot turn,
I feel how in their presence doth abide

AT FLORENCE — FROM M. ANGELO

Light which to God is both the way and guide;
And, kindling at their lustre, if I burn,
My noble fire emits the joyful ray
That through the realms of glory shines for aye.

XXII

AT FLORENCE — FROM M. ANGELO

1837–42   1842

ETERNAL Lord! eased of a cumbrous load,
And loosened from the world, I turn to Thee;
Shun, like a shattered bark, the storm, and flee
To thy protection for a safe abode.
The crown of thorns, hands pierced upon the tree,
The meek, benign, and lacerated face,
To a sincere repentance promise grace,
To the sad soul give hope of pardon free.
With justice mark not Thou, O Light divine,
My fault, nor hear it with thy sacred ear;
Neither put forth that way thy arm severe;
Wash with thy blood my sins; thereto incline
More readily the more my years require
Help, and forgiveness speedy and entire.

XXIII

AMONG THE RUINS OF A CONVENT IN THE APENNINES

1837–42   1842

The political revolutions of our time have multiplied, on the Continent, objects that unavoidably call forth reflections such as are expressed in these verses, but the Ruins in those countries are too recent to exhibit, in anything like an equal degree, the beauty with which time and nature have invested the remains of our Convents and Abbeys. These verses it will be observed take up the beauty long before it is matured, as one cannot but wish it may be among some of the desolations of Italy, France, and Germany.

Ye Trees! whose slender roots entwine
  Altars that piety neglects;
Whose infant arms enclasp the shrine
  Which no devotion now respects;
If not a straggler from the herd
Here ruminate, nor shrouded bird,
Chanting her low-voiced hymn, take pride
In aught that ye would grace or hide —
How sadly is your love misplaced,
Fair Trees, your bounty run to waste!
Ye, too, wild Flowers! that no one heeds,
And ye — full often spurned as weeds —

[115]

MEMORIALS OF A TOUR IN ITALY

In beauty clothed, or breathing sweetness
From fractured arch and mouldering wall —
Do but more touchingly recall
Man's headstrong violence and Time's fleetness,
Making the precincts ye adorn
Appear to sight still more forlorn.

XXIV

IN LOMBARDY

1837–42   1842

SEE, where his difficult way that Old Man wins
Bent by a load of Mulberry leaves! — most hard
Appears *his* lot, to the small Worm's compared,
For whom his toil with early day begins.
Acknowledging no task-master, at will
(As if her labour and her ease were twins)
She seems to work, at pleasure to lie still; —
And softly sleeps within the thread she spins.
So fare they — the Man serving as her Slave.
Ere long their fates do each to each conform:
Both pass into new being, — but the Worm,
Transfigured, sinks into a hopeless grave;
His volant Spirit will, he trusts, ascend
To bliss unbounded, glory without end.

XXV

AFTER LEAVING ITALY

1837-42   1842

I had proof in several instances that the Carbonari, if I may still call them so, and their favourers, are opening their eyes to the necessity of patience, and are intent upon spreading knowledge actively but quietly as they can. May they have resolution to continue in this course! for it is the only one by which they can truly benefit their country. We left Italy by the way which is called the "Nuova Strada d'Alemagna," to the east of the high passes of the Alps, which take you at once from Italy into Switzerland. This road leads across several smaller heights, and winds down different vales in succession, so that it was only by the accidental sound of a few German words that I was aware we had quitted Italy, and hence the unwelcome shock alluded to in the two or three last lines of the latter sonnet.

FAIR Land! Thee all men greet with joy; how few,
Whose souls take pride in freedom, virtue, fame,
Part from thee without pity dyed in shame:
I could not — while from Venice we withdrew,
Led on till an Alpine strait confined our view
Within its depths, and to the shore we came
Of Lago Morto, dreary sight and name,
Which o'er sad thoughts a sadder colouring threw.
Italia! on the surface of thy spirit,

AFTER LEAVING ITALY

(Too aptly emblemed by that torpid lake)
Shall a few partial breezes only creep? —
Be its depths quickened; what thou dost inherit
Of the world's hopes, dare to fulfil; awake,
Mother of Heroes, from thy death-like sleep!

XXVI

CONTINUED

1837 1842

As indignation mastered grief, my tongue
Spake bitter words; words that did ill agree
With those rich stores of Nature's imagery,
And divine Art, that fast to memory clung —
Thy gifts, magnificent Region, ever young
In the sun's eye, and in his sister's sight
How beautiful! how worthy to be sung
In strains of rapture, or subdued delight!
I feign not; witness that unwelcome shock
That followed the first sound of German speech,
Caught the far-winding barrier Alps among.
In that announcement, greeting seemed to mock
Parting; the casual word had power to reach
My heart, and filled that heart with conflict strong.

AT BOLOGNA, IN REMEMBRANCE OF THE LATE INSURRECTIONS, 1837

1837 1842

I

Ah why deceive ourselves! by no mere fit
Of sudden passion roused shall men attain
True freedom where for ages they have lain
Bound in a dark abominable pit,
With life's best sinews more and more unknit.
Here, there, a banded few who loathe the chain
May rise to break it; effort worse than vain
For thee, O great Italian nation, split
Into those jarring fractions. — Let thy scope
Be one fixed mind for all; thy rights approve
To thy own conscience gradually renewed;
Learn to make Time the father of wise Hope;
Then trust thy cause to the arm of Fortitude,
The light of Knowledge, and the warmth of Love.

AT BOLOGNA

II

HARD task! exclaim the undisciplined, to lean
On Patience coupled with such slow endeavour,
That long-lived servitude must last for ever.
Perish the grovelling few, who, prest between
Wrongs and the terror of redress, would wean
Millions from glorious aims. Our chains to sever
Let us break forth in tempest now or never! —
What, is there then no space for golden mean
And gradual progress? — Twilight leads to day,
And, even within the burning zones of earth,
The hastiest sunrise yields a temperate ray;
The softest breeze to fairest flowers gives birth:
Think not that Prudence dwells in dark abodes,
She scans the future with the eye of gods.

AT BOLOGNA

III

As leaves are to the tree whereon they grow
And wither, every human generation
Is, to the Being of a mighty nation,
Locked in our world's embrace through weal and
      woe;
Thought that should teach the zealot to forego
Rash schemes, to abjure all selfish agitation,
And seek through noiseless pains and moderation
The unblemished good they only can bestow.
Alas! with most, who weigh futurity
Against time present, passion holds the scales:
Hence equal ignorance of both prevails,
And nations sink; or, struggling to be free,
Are doomed to flounder on, like wounded whales
Tossed on the bosom of a stormy sea.

"WHAT IF OUR NUMBERS BARELY COULD DEFY"

1837   1837

WHAT if our numbers barely could defy
The arithmetic of babes, must foreign hordes,
Slaves, vile as ever were befooled by words,
Striking through English breasts the anarchy
Of Terror, bear us to the ground, and tie
Our hands behind our backs with felon cords?
Yields every thing to discipline of swords?
Is man as good as man, none low, none high? —
Nor discipline nor valour can withstand
The shock, nor quell the inevitable rout,
When in some great extremity breaks out
A people, on their own beloved Land
Risen, like one man, to combat in the sight
Of a just God for liberty and right.

A NIGHT THOUGHT

1837   1837

These verses were thrown off extempore upon leaving Mrs. Luff's house at Fox-Ghyll, one evening. The good woman is not disposed to look at the bright side of things, and there happened to be present certain ladies who had reached the point of life where *youth* is ended, and who seemed to contend with each other in expressing their dislike of the country and climate. One of them had been heard to say she could not endure a country where there was "neither sunshine nor cavaliers."

Lo! where the Moon along the sky
Sails with her happy destiny;
Oft is she hid from mortal eye
        Or dimly seen,
But when the clouds asunder fly
        How bright her mien!

Far different we — a froward race,
Thousands though rich in Fortune's grace
With cherished sullenness of pace
        Their way pursue,
Ingrates who wear a smileless face
        The whole year through.

[125]

A NIGHT THOUGHT

If kindred humours e'er would make
My spirit droop for drooping's sake,
From Fancy following in thy wake,
    Bright ship of heaven!
A counter impulse let me take
    And be forgiven.

TO THE PLANET VENUS

UPON ITS APPROXIMATION (AS AN EVENING STAR) TO
THE EARTH, JAN. 1838.

1838   1838

WHAT strong allurement draws, what spirit guides,
Thee, Vesper! brightening still, as if the nearer
Thou com'st to man's abode the spot grew dearer
Night after night? True is it Nature hides
Her treasures less and less. — Man now presides
In power, where once he trembled in his weakness;
Science advances with gigantic strides;
But are we aught enriched in love and meekness?
Aught dost thou see, bright Star! of pure and wise
More than in humbler times graced human story;
That makes our hearts more apt to sympathise
With heaven, our souls more fit for future glory,
When earth shall vanish from our closing eyes,
Ere we lie down in our last dormitory?

COMPOSED AT RYDAL ON MAY MORNING, 1838

1838   1838

This and the sonnet entitled "The Pillar of Trajan," p. 646, were composed on what we call the "Far Terrace" at Rydal Mount, where I have murmured out many thousands of verses.

IF with old love of you, dear Hills! I share
New love of many a rival image brought
From far, forgive the wanderings of my thought:
Nor art thou wronged, sweet May! when I compare
Thy present birth-morn with thy last, so fair,
So rich to me in favours. For my lot
Then was, within the famed Egerian Grot
To sit and muse, fanned by its dewy air
Mingling with thy soft breath! That morning too,
Warblers I heard their joy unbosoming
Amid the sunny, shadowy, Colyseum;
Heard them, unchecked by aught of saddening hue,
For victories there won by flower-crowned Spring,
Chant in full choir their innocent Te Deum.

Under the Hawthorn

COMPOSED ON A MAY MORNING, 1838

1838   1838

LIFE with yon Lambs, like day, is just begun,
Yet Nature seems to them a heavenly guide.
Does joy approach? they meet the coming tide;
And sullenness avoid, as now they shun
Pale twilight's lingering glooms, — and in the sun
Couch near their dams, with quiet satisfied;
Or gambol — each with his shadow at his side,
Varying its shape wherever he may run.
As they from turf yet hoar with sleepy dew
All turn, and court the shining and the green,
Where herbs look up, and opening flowers are seen;
Why to God's goodness cannot We be true,
And so, His gifts and promises between,
Feed to the last on pleasures ever new?

"HARK! 'T IS THE THRUSH, UN-DAUNTED, UNDEPREST"

1838   1838

Hark! 't is the Thrush, undaunted, undeprest,
By twilight premature of cloud and rain;
Nor does that roaring wind deaden his strain
Who carols thinking of his Love and nest,
And seems, as more incited, still more blest.
Thanks; thou hast snapped a fireside Prisoner's
        chain,
Exulting Warbler! eased a fretted brain,
And in a moment charmed my cares to rest.
Yes, I will forth, bold Bird! and front the blast,
That we may sing together, if thou wilt,
So loud, so clear, my Partner through life's day,
Mute in her nest love-chosen, if not love-built
Like thine, shall gladden, as in seasons past,
Thrilled by loose snatches of the social Lay.

" 'T IS HE WHOSE YESTER-EVENING'S HIGH DISDAIN"

1838   1838

'T IS He whose yester-evening's high disdain
Beat back the roaring storm — but how subdued
His day-break note, a sad vicissitude!
Does the hour's drowsy weight his glee restrain?
Or, like the nightingale, her joyous vein
Pleased to renounce, does this dear Thrush attune
His voice to suit the temper of yon Moon
Doubly depressed, setting, and in her wane?
Rise, tardy Sun! and let the Songster prove
(The balance trembling between night and morn
No longer) with what ecstasy upborne
He can pour forth his spirit. In heaven above,
And earth below, they best can serve true gladness
Who meet most feelingly the calls of sadness.

"OH WHAT A WRECK! HOW CHANGED IN MIEN AND SPEECH!"

1838(?)   1838

The sad condition of poor Mrs. Southey put me upon writing this. It has afforded comfort to many persons whose friends have been similarly affected.

Oh what a Wreck! how changed in mien and speech!
Yet — though dread Powers, that work in mystery, spin
Entanglings of the brain; though shadows stretch
O'er the chilled heart — reflect; far, far within
Hers is a holy Being, freed from Sin.
She is not what she seems, a forlorn wretch;
But delegated Spirits comfort fetch
To Her from heights that Reason may not win.
Like Children, She is privileged to hold
Divine communion; both do live and move,
Whate'er to shallow Faith their ways unfold,
Inly illumined by Heaven's pitying love;
Love pitying innocence not long to last,
In them — in Her our sins and sorrows past.

A PLEA FOR AUTHORS, MAY 1838

1838   1838

FAILING impartial measure to dispense
To every suitor, Equity is lame;
And social Justice, stript of reverence
For natural rights, a mockery and a shame;
Law but a servile dupe of false pretence,
If, guarding grossest things from common claim
Now and for ever, She, to works that came
From mind and spirit, grudge a short-lived fence.
"What! lengthened privilege, a lineal tie,
 For *Books!*" Yes, heartless Ones, or be it proved
That 't is a fault in Us to have lived and loved
Like others, with like temporal hopes to die;
No public harm that Genius from her course
Be turned; and streams of truth dried up, even at
    their source!

A POET TO HIS GRANDCHILD

SEQUEL TO THE FOREGOING

1838   1838

"Son of my buried Son, while thus thy hand
Is clasping mine, it saddens me to think
How Want may press thee down, and with thee sink
Thy children left unfit, through vain demand
Of culture, even to feel or understand
My simplest Lay that to their memory
May cling; — hard fate! which haply need not be
Did Justice mould the statutes of the Land.
A Book time-cherished and an honoured name
Are high rewards; but bound they Nature's claim
Or Reason's? No — hopes spun in timid line
From out the bosom of a modest home
Extend through unambitious years to come,
My careless Little-one, for thee and thine!"

"BLEST STATESMAN HE, WHOSE MIND'S UNSELFISH WILL"

1838   1838

Blest Statesman He, whose Mind's unselfish will
Leaves him at ease among grand thoughts: whose
    eye
Sees that, apart from magnanimity,
Wisdom exists not; nor the humbler skill
Of Prudence, disentangling good and ill
With patient care. What tho' assaults run high,
They daunt not him who holds his ministry,
Resolute, at all hazards, to fulfil
Its duties; — prompt to move, but firm to wait, —
Knowing, things rashly sought are rarely found;
That, for the functions of an ancient State —
Strong by her charters, free because imbound,
Servant of Providence, not slave of Fate —
Perilous is sweeping change, all chance unsound.

VALEDICTORY SONNET

1838   1838

Closing the Volume of Sonnets published in 1838.

SERVING no haughty Muse, my hands have here
Disposed some cultured Flowerets (drawn from spots
Where they bloomed singly, or in scattered knots),
Each kind in several beds of one parterre;
Both to allure the casual Loiterer,
And that, so placed, my Nurslings may requite
Studious regard with opportune delight,
Nor be unthanked, unless I fondly err.
But metaphor dismissed, and thanks apart,
Reader, farewell! My last words let them be —
If in this book Fancy and Truth agree;
If simple Nature trained by careful Art
Through It have won a passage to thy heart;
Grant me thy love, I crave no other fee!

PROTEST AGAINST THE BALLOT

1838   1838

FORTH rushed from Envy sprung and Self-conceit,
A Power misnamed the SPIRIT of REFORM,
And through the astonished Island swept in storm,
Threatening to lay all orders at her feet
That crossed her way. Now stoops she to entreat
Licence to hide at intervals her head
Where she may work, safe, undisquieted,
In a close Box, covert for Justice meet.
St. George of England! keep a watchful eye
Fixed on the Suitor; frustrate her request —
Stifle her hope; for, if the State comply,
From such Pandorian gift may come a Pest
Worse than the Dragon that bowed low his crest,
Pierced by thy spear in glorious victory.

SONNETS

UPON THE PUNISHMENT OF DEATH
IN SERIES

I

1839–40 1841

SUGGESTED BY THE VIEW OF LANCASTER CASTLE
(ON THE ROAD FROM THE SOUTH)

THIS Spot — at once unfolding sight so fair
Of sea and land, with yon grey towers that still
Rise up as if to lord it over air —
Might soothe in human breasts the sense of ill,
Or charm it out of memory; yea, might fill
The heart with joy and gratitude to God
For all his bounties upon man bestowed:
Why bears it then the name of "Weeping Hill"?
Thousands, as toward yon old Lancastrian Towers,
A prison's crown, along this way they past
For lingering durance or quick death with shame,
From this bare eminence thereon have cast
Their first look — blinded as tears fell in showers
Shed on their chains; and hence that doleful name.

[138]

UPON THE PUNISHMENT OF DEATH

II

TENDERLY do we feel by Nature's law
For worst offenders: though the heart will heave
With indignation, deeply moved we grieve,
In after thought, for Him who stood in awe
Neither of God nor man, and only saw,
Lost wretch, a horrible device enthroned
On proud temptations, till the victim groaned
Under the steel his hand had dared to draw.
But oh, restrain compassion, if its course,
As oft befalls, prevent or turn aside
Judgments and aims and acts whose higher source
Is sympathy with the unforewarned, who died
Blameless — with them that shuddered o'er his
            grave,
And all who from the law firm safety crave.

[139]

III

THE Roman Consul doomed his sons to die
Who had betrayed their country. The stern word
Afforded (may it through all time afford)
A theme for praise and admiration high.
Upon the surface of humanity
He rested not; its depths his mind explored;
He felt; but his parental bosom's lord
Was Duty, — Duty calmed his agony.
And some, we know, when they by wilful act
A single human life have wrongly taken,
Pass sentence on themselves, confess the fact,
And, to atone for it, with soul unshaken
Kneel at the feet of Justice, and, for faith
Broken with all mankind, solicit death.

UPON THE PUNISHMENT OF DEATH

IV

Is *Death,* when evil against good has fought
With such fell mastery that a man may dare
By deeds the blackest purpose to lay bare;
Is Death, for one to that condition brought,
For him, or any one, the thing that ought
To be *most* dreaded? Lawgivers, beware,
Lest, capital pains remitting till ye spare
The murderer, ye, by sanction to that thought
Seemingly given, debase the general mind;
Tempt the vague will tried standards to disown,
Nor only palpable restraints unbind,
But upon Honour's head disturb the crown,
Whose absolute rule permits not to withstand
In the weak love of life his least command.

V

NOT to the object specially designed,
Howe'er momentous in itself it be,
Good to promote or curb depravity,
Is the wise Legislator's view confined.
His Spirit, when most severe, is oft most kind;
As all Authority in earth depends
On Love and Fear, their several powers he blends,
Copying with awe the one Paternal mind.
Uncaught by processes in show humane,
He feels how far the act would derogate
From even the humblest functions of the State;
If she, self-shorn of Majesty, ordain
That never more shall hang upon her breath
The last alternative of Life or Death.

UPON THE PUNISHMENT OF DEATH

VI

Ye brood of conscience — Spectres! that frequent
The bad Man's restless walk, and haunt his bed —
Fiends in your aspect, yet beneficent
In act, as hovering Angels when they spread
Their wings to guard the unconscious Innocent —
Slow be the Statutes of the land to share
A laxity that could not but impair
Your power to punish crime, and so prevent.
And ye, Beliefs! coiled serpent-like about
The adage on all tongues, "Murder will out,"
How shall your ancient warnings work for good
In the full might they hitherto have shown,
If for deliberate shedder of man's blood
Survive not Judgment that requires his own?

VII

BEFORE the world had past her time of youth
While polity and discipline were weak,
The precept eye for eye, and tooth for tooth,
Came forth — a light, though but as of daybreak,
Strong as could then be borne.   A Master meek
Proscribed the spirit fostered by that rule,
Patience *his* law, long-suffering *his* school,
And love the end, which all through peace must seek.
But lamentably do they err who strain
His mandates, given rash impulse to control
And keep vindictive thirstings from the soul,
So far that, if consistent in their scheme,
They must forbid the State to inflict a pain,
Making of social order a mere dream.

VIII

FIT retribution, by the moral code
Determined, lies beyond the State's embrace,
Yet, as she may, for each peculiar case
She plants well-measured terrors in the road
Of wrongful acts. Downward it is and broad,
And, the main fear once doomed to banishment,
Far oftener then, bad ushering worse event,
Blood would be spilt that in his dark abode
Crime might lie better hid. And, should the change
Take from the horror due to a foul deed,
Pursuit and evidence so far must fail,
And, guilt escaping, passion then might plead
In angry spirits for her old free range,
And the "wild justice of revenge" prevail.

SONNETS

IX

Though to give timely warning and deter
Is one great aim of penalty, extend
Thy mental vision further and ascend
Far higher, else full surely shalt thou err.
What is a State? The wise behold in her
A creature born of time, that keeps one eye
Fixed on the statutes of Eternity,
To which her judgments reverently defer.
Speaking through Law's dispassionate voice the
     State
Endues her conscience with external life
And being, to prelude or quell the strife
Of individual will, to elevate
The grovelling mind, the erring to recall,
And fortify the moral sense of all.

UPON THE PUNISHMENT OF DEATH

X

Our bodily life, some plead, that life the shrine
Of an immortal spirit, is a gift
So sacred, so informed with light divine,
That no tribunal, though most wise to sift
Deed and intent, should turn the Being adrift
Into that world where penitential tear
May not avail, nor prayer have for God's ear
A voice — that world whose veil no hand can lift
For earthly sight. "Eternity and Time,"
They urge, "have interwoven claims and rights
Not to be jeopardised through foulest crime:
The sentence rule by mercy's heaven-born lights."
Even so; but measuring not by finite sense
Infinite Power, perfect Intelligence.

XI

Ah, think how one compelled for life to abide
Locked in a dungeon needs must eat the heart
Out of his own humanity, and part
With every hope that mutual cares provide;
And, should a less unnatural doom confide
In life-long exile on a savage coast,
Soon the relapsing penitent may boast
Of yet more heinous guilt, with fiercer pride.
Hence thoughtful Mercy, Mercy sage and pure,
Sanctions the forfeiture that Law demands,
Leaving the final issue in *His* hands
Whose goodness knows no change, whose love is
    sure,
Who sees, foresees; who cannot judge amiss,
And wafts at will the contrite soul to bliss.

XII

SEE the Condemned alone within his cell
And prostrate at some moment when remorse
Stings to the quick, and, with resistless force,
Assaults the pride she strove in vain to quell.
Then mark him, him who could so long rebel,
The crime confessed, a kneeling Penitent
Before the Altar, where the Sacrament
Softens his heart, till from his eyes outwell
Tears of salvation. Welcome death! while Heaven
Does in this change exceedingly rejoice;
While yet the solemn heed the State hath given
Helps him to meet the last Tribunal's voice,
In faith, which fresh offences, were he cast
On old temptations, might for ever blast.

XIII

CONCLUSION

Yes, though He well may tremble at the sound
Of his own voice, who from the judgment-seat
Sends the pale Convict to his last retreat
In death; though Listeners shudder all around,
They know the dread requital's source profound;
Nor is, they feel, its wisdom obsolete —
(Would that it were!) the sacrifice unmeet
For Christian Faith. But hopeful signs abound;
The social rights of man breathe purer air,
Religion deepens her preventive care;
Then, moved by needless fear of past abuse,
Strike not from Law's firm hand that awful rod,
But leave it thence to drop for lack of use:
Oh, speed the blessèd hour, Almighty God!

XIV

APOLOGY

THE formal World relaxes her cold chain
For One who speaks in numbers; ampler scope
His utterance finds; and, conscious of the gain,
Imagination works with bolder hope
The cause of grateful reason to sustain;
And, serving Truth, the heart more strongly beats
Against all barriers which his labour meets
In lofty place, or humble Life's domain.
Enough; — before us lay a painful road,
And guidance have I sought in duteous love
From Wisdom's heavenly Father. Hence hath flowed
Patience, with trust that, whatsoe'er the way
Each takes in this high matter, all may move
Cheered with the prospect of a brighter day.

ON A PORTRAIT OF I. F., PAINTED BY MARGARET GILLIES

1840 1851

WE gaze — nor grieve to think that we must die,
But that the precious love this friend hath sown
Within our hearts, the love whose flower hath blown
Bright as if heaven were ever in its eye,
Will pass so soon from human memory;
And not by strangers to our blood alone,
But by our best descendants be unknown,
Unthought of — this may surely claim a sigh.
Yet, blessed Art, we yield not to dejection;
Thou against Time so feelingly dost strive.
Where'er, preserved in this most true reflection,
An image of her soul is kept alive,
Some lingering fragrance of the pure affection,
Whose flower with us will vanish, must survive.

TO I. F.

1840   1851

THE star which comes at close of day to shine
More heavenly bright than when it leads the morn,
Is friendship's emblem, whether the forlorn
She visiteth, or, shedding light benign
Through shades that solemnize Life's calm decline,
Doth make the happy happier. This have we
Learnt, Isabel, from thy society,
Which now we too unwillingly resign
Though for brief absence. But farewell! the page
Glimmers before my sight through thankful tears,
Such as start forth, not seldom, to approve
Our truth, when we, old yet unchilled by age,
Call thee, though known but for a few fleet years,
The heart-affianced sister of our love!

POOR ROBIN [16]

1840 1842

I often ask myself what will become of Rydal Mount after
our day. Will the old walls and steps remain in front of the
house and about the grounds, or will they be swept away with
all the beautiful mosses and ferns and wild geraniums and
other flowers which their rude construction suffered and en-
couraged to grow among them? — This little wild flower —
"Poor Robin" — is here constantly courting my attention,
and exciting what may be called a domestic interest with
the varying aspects of its stalks and leaves and flowers.
Strangely do the tastes of men differ according to their employ-
ment and habits of life. "What a nice well would that be,"
said a labouring man to me one day, "if all that rubbish was
cleared off." The "*rubbish*" was some of the most beautiful
mosses and lichens and ferns and other wild growths that
could possibly be seen. Defend us from the tyranny of trim-
ness and neatness showing itself in this way! Chatterton says
of freedom — "Upon her head wild weeds were spread " ; and
depend upon it if "the marvellous boy" had undertaken to
give Flora a garland, he would have preferred what we are apt
to call weeds to garden-flowers. True taste has an eye for both.
Weeds have been called flowers out of place. I fear the place
most people would assign to them is too limited. Let them
come near to our abodes, as surely they may without impro-
priety or disorder.

Now when the primrose makes a splendid show,
And lilies face the March-winds in full blow,

POOR ROBIN

And humbler growths as moved with one desire
Put on, to welcome spring, their best attire,
Poor Robin is yet flowerless; but how gay
With his red stalks upon this sunny day!
And, as his tufts of leaves he spreads, content
With a hard bed and scanty nourishment,
Mixed with the green, some shine not lacking power
To rival summer's brightest scarlet flower;
And flowers they well might seem to passers-by
If looked at only with a careless eye;
Flowers — or a richer produce (did it suit
The season) sprinklings of ripe strawberry fruit.
But while a thousand pleasures come unsought,
Why fix upon his wealth or want a thought?
Is the string touched in prelude to a lay
Of pretty fancies that would round him play
When all the world acknowledged elfin sway?
Or does it suit our humour to commend
Poor Robin as a sure and crafty friend,
Whose practice teaches, spite of names, to show
Bright colours whether they deceive or no? —
Nay, we would simply praise the free good-will
With which, though slighted, he, on naked hill
Or in warm valley, seeks his part to fill;
Cheerful alike if bare of flowers as now,
Or when his tiny gems shall deck his brow:

POOR ROBIN

Yet more, we wish that men by men despised,
And such as lift their foreheads overprized,
Should sometimes think, where'er they chance to
    spy
This child of Nature's own humility,
What recompence is kept in store or left
For all that seem neglected or bereft;
With what nice care equivalents are given,
How just, how bountiful, the hand of Heaven.

ON A PORTRAIT OF THE DUKE OF WELLINGTON UPON THE FIELD OF WATERLOO, BY HAYDON

1840 1842

This was composed while I was ascending Helvellyn in company with my daughter and her husband. She was on horseback and rode to the top of the hill without once dismounting, a feat which it was scarcely possible to perform except during a season of dry weather; and a guide, with whom we fell in on the mountain, told us he believed it had never been accomplished before by any one.

By Art's bold privilege Warrior and War-horse stand
On ground yet strewn with their last battle's wreck;
Let the Steed glory while his Master's hand
Lies fixed for ages on his conscious neck;
But by the Chieftain's look, though at his side
Hangs that day's treasured sword, how firm a check
Is given to triumph and all human pride!
Yon trophied Mound shrinks to a shadowy speck
In his calm presence! Him the mighty deed
Elates not, brought far nearer the grave's rest,
As shows that time-worn face, for he such seed
Has sown as yields, we trust, the fruit of fame
In Heaven; hence no one blushes for thy name,
Conqueror, 'mid some sad thoughts, divinely blest'

TO A PAINTER

1841(?)   1842

The picture which gave occasion to this and the following
Sonnet was from the pencil of Miss M. Gillies, who resided for
several weeks under our roof at Rydal Mount.

ALL praise the Likeness by thy skill portrayed;
But 't is a fruitless task to paint for me,
Who, yielding not to changes Time has made,
By the habitual light of memory see
Eyes unbedimmed, see bloom that cannot fade,
And smiles that from their birth-place ne'er shall flee
Into the land where ghosts and phantoms be;
And, seeing this, own nothing in its stead.
Couldst thou go back into far-distant years,
Or share with me, fond thought! that inward eye,
Then, and then only, Painter! could thy Art
The visual powers of Nature satisfy,
Which hold, whate'er to common sight appears,
Their sovereign empire in a faithful heart.

ON THE SAME SUBJECT

1841   1842

THOUGH I beheld at first with blank surprise
This Work, I now have gazed on it so long
I see its truth with unreluctant eyes;
O, my Belovèd! I have done thee wrong,
Conscious of blessedness, but, whence it sprung,
Ever too heedless, as I now perceive:
Morn into noon did pass, noon into eve,
And the old day was welcome as the young,
As welcome, and as beautiful — in sooth
More beautiful, as being a thing more holy:
Thanks to thy virtues, to the eternal youth
Of all thy goodness, never melancholy;
To thy large heart and humble mind, that cast
Into one vision, future, present, past.

"WHEN SEVERN'S SWEEPING FLOOD HAD OVERTHROWN"

1842   1842

WHEN Severn's sweeping flood had overthrown
St. Mary's Church, the preacher then would cry: —
"Thus, Christian people, God his might hath shown
That ye to him your love may testify;
Haste, and rebuild the pile." — But not a stone
Resumed its place. Age after age went by,
And Heaven still lacked its due, though piety
In secret did, we trust, her loss bemoan.
But now her Spirit hath put forth its claim
In Power, and Poesy would lend her voice;
Let the new Church be worthy of its aim,
That in its beauty Cardiff may rejoice!
Oh! in the past if cause there was for shame,
Let not our times halt in their better choice.

"INTENT ON GATHERING WOOL FROM HEDGE AND BRAKE"

1842   1842

Suggested by a conversation with Miss Fenwick, who along with her sister had during their childhood, found much delight in such gatherings for the purposes here alluded to.

INTENT on gathering wool from hedge and brake
Yon busy Little-ones rejoice that soon
A poor old Dame will bless them for the boon:
Great is their glee while flake they add to flake
With rival earnestness; far other strife
Than will hereafter move them, if they make
Pastime their idol, give their day of life
To pleasure snatched for reckless pleasure's sake.
Can pomp and show allay one heart-born grief?
Pains which the World inflicts can she requite?
Not for an interval however brief;
The silent thoughts that search for stedfast light,
Love from her depths, and Duty in her might,
And Faith — these only yield secure relief.

PRELUDE

PREFIXED TO THE VOLUME ENTITLED "POEMS CHIEFLY
OF EARLY AND LATE YEARS"

1842   1842

These verses were begun while I was on a visit to my son
John at Brigham, and were finished at Rydal. As the con-
tents of the volume, to which they are now prefixed, will be
assigned to their respective classes when my poems shall be col-
lected in one volume, I should be at a loss where with propriety
to place this prelude, being too restricted in its bearing to
serve for a preface for the whole. The lines towards the con-
clusion allude to the discontents then fomented through the
country by the agitators of the Anti-Corn-Law League: the
particular causes of such troubles are transitory, but disposi-
tion to excite and liability to be excited are nevertheless per-
manent, and therefore proper objects for the poet's regard.

In desultory walk through orchard grounds,
Or some deep chestnut grove, oft have I paused
The while a Thrush, urged rather than restrained
By gusts of vernal storm, attuned his song
To his own genial instincts; and was heard
(Though not without some plaintive tones between)
To utter, above showers of blossom swept
From tossing boughs, the promise of a calm,
Which the unsheltered traveller might receive
With thankful spirit. The descant, and the wind

PRELUDE

That seemed to play with it in love or scorn,
Encouraged and endeared the strain of words
That haply flowed from me, by fits of silence
Impelled to livelier pace. But now, my Book!
Charged with those lays, and others of like mood,
Or loftier pitch if higher rose the theme,
Go, single — yet aspiring to be joined
With thy Forerunners that through many a year
Have faithfully prepared each other's way —
Go forth upon a mission best fulfilled
When and wherever, in this changeful world,
Power hath been given to please for higher ends
Than pleasure only; gladdening to prepare
For wholesome sadness, troubling to refine,
Calming to raise; and, by a sapient Art
Diffused through all the mysteries of our Being,
Softening the toils and pains that have not ceased
To cast their shadows on our mother Earth
Since the primeval doom. Such is the grace
Which, though unsued for, fails not to descend
With heavenly inspiration; such the aim
That Reason dictates; and, as even the wish
Has virtue in it, why should hope to me
Be wanting that sometimes, where fancied ills
Harass the mind and strip from off the bowers
Of private life their natural pleasantness,

PRELUDE

A Voice — devoted to the love whose seeds
Are sown in every human breast, to beauty
Lodged within compass of the humblest sight,
To cheerful intercourse with wood and field,
And sympathy with man's substantial griefs —
Will not be heard in vain? And in those days
When unforeseen distress spreads far and wide
Among a People mournfully cast down,
Or into anger roused by venal words
In recklessness flung out to overturn
The judgment, and divert the general heart
From mutual good — some strain of thine, my Book!
Caught at propitious intervals, may win
Listeners who not unwillingly admit
Kindly emotion tending to console
And reconcile; and both with young and old
Exalt the sense of thoughtful gratitude
For benefits that still survive, by faith
In progress, under laws divine, maintained.

FLOATING ISLAND

1842 1842

.My poor sister takes a pleasure in repeating these verses, which she composed not long before the beginning of her sad illness.

These lines are by the author of the "Address to the Wind," etc., published heretofore along with my Poems.

HARMONIOUS Powers with Nature work
On sky, earth, river, lake and sea;
Sunshine and cloud, whirlwind and breeze,
All in one duteous task agree.

Once did I see a slip of earth
(By throbbing waves long undermined)
Loosed from its hold; how, no one knew,
But all might see it float, obedient to the wind;

Might see it, from the mossy shore
Dissevered, float upon the Lake,
Float with its crest of trees adorned
On which the warbling birds their pastime take.

Food, shelter, safety, there they find;
There berries ripen, flowerets bloom;

[165]

FLOATING ISLAND

There insects live their lives, and die;
A peopled world it is; in size a tiny room.

And thus through many seasons' space
This little Island may survive;
But Nature, though we mark her not,
Will take away, may cease to give.

Perchance when you are wandering forth
Upon some vacant sunny day,
Without an object, hope, or fear,
Thither your eyes may turn — the Isle is passed
away;

Buried beneath the glittering Lake,
Its place no longer to be found;
Yet the lost fragments shall remain
To fertilize some other ground.

"THE CRESCENT-MOON, THE STAR OF LOVE"

1842   1842

THE Crescent-moon, the Star of Love,
  Glories of evening, as ye there are seen
  With but a span of sky between —
  Speak one of you, my doubts remove,
Which is the attendant Page and which the Queen?

TO A REDBREAST — (IN SICKNESS)

(?) 1842

Almost the only verses by our lamented Sister Sara Hutch-
inson.

STAY, little cheerful Robin! stay,
　And at my casement sing,
Though it should prove a farewell lay
　And this our parting spring.

Though I, alas! may ne'er enjoy
　The promise in thy song;
A charm, *that* thought can not destroy,
　Doth to thy strain belong.

Methinks that in my dying hour
　Thy song would still be dear,
And with a more than earthly power
　My passing Spirit cheer.

Then, little Bird, this boon confer,
　Come, and my requiem sing,
Nor fail to be the harbinger
　Of everlasting Spring.

MISCELLANEOUS SONNETS

1842(?)   1842

I

I was impelled to write this Sonnet by the disgusting frequency with which the word *artistical*, imported with other impertinences from the Germans, is employed by writers of the present day: for artistical let them substitute artificial, and the poetry written on this system, both at home and abroad, will be for the most part much better characterised.

A POET! — He hath put his heart to school,
Nor dares to move unpropped upon the staff
Which Art hath lodged within his hand — must laugh
By precept only, and shed tears by rule.
Thy Art be Nature; the live current quaff,
And let the groveller sip his stagnant pool,
In fear that else, when Critics grave and cool
Have killed him, Scorn should write his epitaph.
How does the Meadow-flower its bloom unfold?
Because the lovely little flower is free
Down to its root, and, in that freedom, bold;
And so the grandeur of the Forest-tree
Comes not by casting in a formal mould,
But from its *own* divine vitality.

II

Hundreds of times have I seen, hanging about and above the vale of Rydal, clouds that might have given birth to this Sonnet, which was thrown off on the impulse of the moment one evening when I was returning home from the favourite walk of ours, along the Rotha, under Loughrigg.

THE most alluring clouds that mount the sky
Owe to a troubled element their forms,
Their hues to sunset. If with raptured eye
We watch their splendour, shall we covet storms,
And wish the Lord of day his slow decline
Would hasten, that such pomp may float on high?
Behold, already they forget to shine,
Dissolve — and leave, to him who gazed, a sigh.
Not loth to thank each moment for its boon
Of pure delight, come whencesoe'er it may,
Peace let us seek, — to stedfast things attune
Calm expectations — leaving to the gay
And volatile their love of transient bowers,
The house that cannot pass away be ours.

Evening on Rydal after Rain

III

This Sonnet is recommended to the perusal of all those who consider that the evils under which we groan are to be removed or palliated by measures ungoverned by moral and religious principles.

FEEL for the wrongs to universal ken
Daily exposed, woe that unshrouded lies;
And seek the Sufferer in his darkest den,
Whether conducted to the spot by sighs
And moanings, or he dwells (as if the wren
Taught him concealment) hidden from all eyes
In silence and the awful modesties
Of sorrow; — feel for all, as brother Men!
Rest not in hope want's icy chain to thaw
By casual boons and formal charities;
Learn to be just, just through impartial law;
Far as ye may, erect and equalise;
And, what ye cannot reach by statute, draw
Each from his fountain of self-sacrifice!

IV

IN ALLUSION TO VARIOUS RECENT HISTORIES AND NOTICES OF THE FRENCH REVOLUTION

PORTENTOUS change when History can appear
As the cool Advocate of foul device;
Reckless audacity extol, and jeer
At consciences perplexed with scruples nice!
They who bewail not, must abhor, the sneer
Born of Conceit, Power's blind Idolater;
Or haply sprung from vaunting Cowardice
Betrayed by mockery of holy fear.
Hath it not long been said the wrath of Man
Works not the righteousness of God? Oh bend,
Bend, ye Perverse! to judgments from on High,
Laws that lay under Heaven's perpetual ban,
All principles of action that transcend
The sacred limits of humanity.

V

CONTINUED

Who ponders National events shall find
An awful balancing of loss and gain,
Joy based on sorrow, good with ill combined,
And proud deliverance issuing out of pain
And direful throes; as if the All-ruling Mind,
With whose perfection it consists to ordain
Volcanic burst, earthquake, and hurricane,
Dealt in like sort with feeble human kind
By laws immutable. But woe for him
Who thus deceived shall lend an eager hand
To social havoc. Is not Conscience ours,
And Truth, whose eye guilt only can make dim;
And Will, whose office, by divine command,
Is to control and check disordered Powers?

VI

CONCLUDED

LONG-FAVOURED England! be not thou misled
By monstrous theories of alien growth,
Lest alien frenzy seize thee, waxing wroth,
Self-smitten till thy garments reek dyed red
With thy own blood, which tears in torrents shed
Fail to wash out, tears flowing ere thy troth
Be plighted, not to ease but sullen sloth,
Or wan despair — the ghost of false hope fled
Into a shameful grave. Among thy youth,
My Country! if such warning be held dear,
Then shall a Veteran's heart be thrilled with joy,
One who would gather from eternal truth,
For time and season, rules that work to cheer —
Not scourge, to save the People — not destroy.

VII

MEN of the Western World! in Fate's dark book
Whence these opprobrious leaves of dire portent?
Think ye your British Ancestors forsook
Their native Land, for outrage provident;
From unsubmissive necks the bridle shook
To give, in their Descendants, freer vent
And wider range to passions turbulent,
To mutual tyranny a deadlier look?
Nay, said a voice, soft as the south wind's breath,
Dive through the stormy surface of the flood
To the great current flowing underneath;
Explore the countless springs of silent good;
So shall the truth be better understood,
And thy grieved Spirit brighten strong in faith.[17]

VIII

Lo! where she stands fixed in a saint-like trance,
One upward hand, as if she needed rest
From rapture, lying softly on her breast!
Nor wants her eyeball an ethereal glance;
But not the less — nay more — that countenance,
While thus illumined, tells of painful strife
For a sick heart made weary of this life
By love, long crossed with adverse circumstance.
— Would She were now as when she hoped to pass
At God's appointed hour to them who tread
Heaven's sapphire pavement, yet breathed well con-
    tent,
Well pleased, her foot should print earth's common
    grass,
Lived thankful for day's light, for daily bread,
For health, and time in obvious duty spent.

THE NORMAN BOY

1842   1842

The subject of this poem was sent me by Mrs. Ogle, to whom I was personally unknown, with a hope on her part that I might be induced to relate the incident in verse; and I do not regret that I took the trouble; for not improbably the fact is illustrative of the boy's early piety, and may concur with my other little pieces on children to produce profitable reflection among my youthful readers. This is said however with an absolute conviction that children will derive most benefit from books which are not unworthy the perusal of persons of any age. I protest with my whole heart against those productions, so abundant in the present day, in which the doings of children are dwelt upon as if they were incapable of being interested in anything else. On this subject I have dwelt at length in the poem on the growth of my own mind.

HIGH on a broad unfertile tract of forest-skirted Down,
Nor kept by Nature for herself, nor made by man his
    own,
From home and company remote and every playful joy,
Served, tending a few sheep and goats, a ragged Nor-
    man Boy.

Him never saw I, nor the spot; but from an English
    Dame,
Stranger to me and yet my friend, a simple notice came,

With suit that I would speak in verse of that seques-
 tered child
Whom, one bleak winter's day, she met upon the dreary
 Wild.

His flock, along the woodland's edge with relics sprinkled
 o'er
Of last night's snow, beneath a sky threatening the fall
 of more,
Where tufts of herbage tempted each, were busy at
 their feed,
And the poor Boy was busier still, with work of anxious
 heed.

There *was* he, where of branches rent and withered and
 decayed,
For covert from the keen north wind, his hands a hut
 had made.
A tiny tenement, forsooth, and frail, as needs must be
A thing of such materials framed, by a builder such as
 he.

The hut stood finished by his pains, nor seemingly
 lacked aught
That skill or means of his could add, but the architect
 had wrought

Sheep in Winter

THE NORMAN BOY

Some limber twigs into a Cross, well-shaped with fingers
    nice,
To be engrafted on the top of his small edifice.

That Cross he now was fastening there, as the surest
    power and best
For supplying all deficiencies, all wants of the rude
    nest
In which, from burning heat, or tempest driving far and
    wide,
The innocent Boy, else shelterless, his lonely head must
    hide.

That Cross belike he also raised as a standard for the
    true
And faithful service of his heart in the worst that might
    ensue
Of hardship and distressful fear, amid the houseless
    waste
Where he, in his poor self so weak, by Providence was
    placed.

—— Here, Lady! might I cease; but nay, let *us* before
    we part
With this dear holy shepherd-boy breathe a prayer of
    earnest heart,

That unto him, where'er shall lie his life's appointed
    way,
The Cross, fixed in his soul, may prove an all-sufficing
    stay.

THE POET'S DREAM

SEQUEL TO THE NORMAN BOY

1842   1842

JUST as those final words were penned, the sun broke
    out in power,
And gladdened all things; but, as chanced, within that
    very hour,
Air blackened, thunder growled, fire flashed from clouds
    that hid the sky,
And, for the Subject of my Verse, I heaved a pensive
    sigh.

Nor could my heart by second thoughts from heaviness
    be cleared,
For bodied forth before my eyes the cross-crowned hut
    appeared;
And, while around it storm as fierce seemed troubling
    earth and air,
I saw, within, the Norman Boy kneeling alone in prayer.

The Child, as if the thunder's voice spake with articu-
    late call,
Bowed meekly in submissive fear, before the Lord of
    All;

His lips were moving; and his eyes, upraised to sue for
    grace,
With soft illumination cheered the dimness of that place.

How beautiful is holiness! — what wonder if the sight,
Almost as vivid as a dream, produced a dream at night?
It came with sleep and showed the Boy, no cherub, not
    transformed.
But the poor ragged Thing whose ways my human heart
    had warmed.

Me had the dream equipped with wings, so I took him in
    my arms,
And lifted from the grassy floor, stilling his faint alarms,
And bore him high through yielding air my debt of love
    to pay,
By giving him, for both our sakes, an hour of holiday.

I whispered, "Yet a little while, dear Child! thou art
    my own,
To show thee some delightful thing, in country or in
    town.
What shall it be? a mirthful throng? or that holy place
    and calm
St. Denis, filled with royal tombs, or the Church of
    Notre Dame?

THE POET'S DREAM

"St. Ouen's golden Shrine? Or choose what else would
please thee most

Of any wonder Normandy, or all proud France, can
boast!"

"My Mother," said the Boy, "was born near to a
blessèd Tree,

The Chapel Oak of Allonville,[18] good Angel, show it
me!"

On wings, from broad and stedfast poise let loose by this
reply,

For Allonville, o'er down and dale, away then did we
fly;

O'er town and tower we flew, and fields in May's fresh
verdure drest;

The wings they did not flag; the Child, though grave,
was not deprest.

But who shall show, to waking sense, the gleam of light
that broke

Forth from his eyes, when first the Boy looked down on
that huge oak,

For length of days so much revered, so famous where it
stands

For twofold hallowing — Nature's care, and work of
human hands?

[183]

Strong as an Eagle with my charge I glided round and
    round
The wide-spread boughs, for view of door, window, and
    stair that wound
Gracefully up the gnarlèd trunk; nor left we unsur-
    veyed
The pointed steeple peering forth from the centre of the
    shade.

I lighted — opened with soft touch the chapel's iron
    door,
Past softly, leading in the Boy; and, while from roof to
    floor
From floor to roof all round his eyes the Child with
    wonder cast,
Pleasure on pleasure crowded in, each livelier than the
    last.

For, deftly framed within the trunk, the sanctuary
    showed,
By light of lamp and precious stones, that glimmered
    here, there glowed,
Shrine, Altar, Image, Offerings hung in sign of grati-
    tude;
Sight that inspired accordant thoughts; and speech I
    thus renewed:

THE POET'S DREAM

"Hither the Afflicted come, as thou hast heard thy
    Mother say,
And, kneeling, supplication make to our Lady de la
    Paix;
What mournful sighs have here been heard, and, when
    the voice was stopt
By sudden pangs; what bitter tears have on this pave-
    ment dropt!

"Poor Shepherd of the naked Down, a favoured lot is
    thine,
Far happier lot, dear Boy, than brings full many to this
    shrine;
From body pains and pains of soul thou needest no re-
    lease,
Thy hours as they flow on are spent, if not in joy, in
    peace.

"Then offer up thy heart to God in thankfulness and
    praise,
Give to Him prayers, and many thoughts, in thy most
    busy days;
And in His sight the fragile Cross, on thy small hut, will
    be
Holy as that which long hath crowned the Chapel of
    this Tree;

"Holy as that far seen which crowns the sumptuous
    Church in Rome
Where thousands meet to worship God under a mighty
    Dome;
He sees the bending multitude, he hears the choral
    rites,
Yet not the less, in children's hymns and lonely prayer,
    delights.

"God for his service needeth not proud work of human
    skill;
They please him best who labour most to do in peace his
    will:
So let us strive to live, and to our Spirits will be
    given
Such wings as, when our Saviour calls, shall bear us up
    to heaven."

The Boy no answer made by words, but, so earnest was
    his look,
Sleep fled, and with it fled the dream — recorded in this
    book,
Lest all that passed should melt away in silence from my
    mind,
As visions still more bright have done, and left no trace
    behind.

THE POET'S DREAM

But oh! that Country-man of thine, whose eye, loved
    Child, can see
A pledge of endless bliss in acts of early piety,
In verse, which to thy ear might come, would treat this
    simple theme,
Nor leave untold our happy flight in that adventurous
    dream.

Alas the dream, to thee, poor Boy! to thee from whom it
    flowed,
Was nothing, scarcely can be aught, yet 't was boun-
    teously bestowed,
If I may dare to cherish hope that gentle eyes will read
Not loth, and listening Little-ones, heart-touched, their
    fancies feed.

THE WIDOW ON WINDERMERE SIDE

1842   1842

The facts recorded in this Poem were given me, and the character of the person described, by my friend the Rev. R. P. Graves, who has long officiated as curate at Bowness, to the great benefit of the parish and neighbourhood. The individual was well known to him. She died before these verses were composed. It is scarcely worth while to notice that the stanzas are written in the sonnet form, which was adopted when I thought the matter might be included in twenty-eight lines.

I

How beautiful when up a lofty height
Honour ascends among the humblest poor,
And feeling sinks as deep! See there the door
Of One, a Widow, left beneath a weight
Of blameless debt. On evil Fortune's spite
She wasted no complaint, but strove to make
A just repayment, both for conscience-sake
And that herself and hers should stand upright
In the world's eye. Her work when daylight failed
Paused not, and through the depth of night she kept
Such earnest vigils, that belief prevailed
With some, the noble Creature never slept;
But, one by one, the hand of death assailed
Her children from her inmost heart bewept.

THE WIDOW ON WINDERMERE SIDE

II

The Mother mourned, nor ceased her tears to flow,
Till a winter's noonday placed her buried Son
Before her eyes, last child of many gone —
His raiment of angelic white, and lo!
His very feet bright as the dazzling snow
Which they are touching; yea far brighter, even
As that which comes, or seems to come, from heaven,
Surpasses aught these elements can show.
Much she rejoiced, trusting that from that hour
Whate'er befell she could not grieve or pine;
But the Transfigured, in and out of season,
Appeared, and spiritual presence gained a power
Over material forms that mastered reason.
Oh, gracious Heaven, in pity make her thine!

III

But why that prayer? as if to her could come
No good but by the way that leads to bliss
Through Death, — so judging we should judge amiss.
Since reason failed want is her threatened doom,
Yet frequent transports mitigate the gloom:
Nor of those maniacs is she one that kiss
The air or laugh upon a precipice
No, passing through strange sufferings toward the tomb
She smiles as if a martyr's crown were won:

THE WIDOW ON WINDERMERE SIDE

Oft, when light breaks through clouds or waving trees,
With outspread arms and fallen upon her knees
The Mother hails in her descending Son
An Angel, and in earthly ecstasies
Her own angelic glory seems begun.

Airey Force Valley

AIREY-FORCE VALLEY

1842(?) 1842

—— Not a breath of air
Ruffles the bosom of this leafy glen.
From the brook's margin, wide around, the trees
Are stedfast as the rocks; the brook itself,
Old as the hills that feed it from afar,
Doth rather deepen than disturb the calm
Where all things else are still and motionless.
And yet, even now, a little breeze, perchance
Escaped from boisterous winds that rage without,
Has entered, by the sturdy oaks unfelt,
But to its gentle touch how sensitive
Is the light ash! that, pendant from the brow
Of yon dim cave, in seeming silence makes
A soft eye-music of slow-waving boughs,
Powerful almost as vocal harmony
To stay the wanderer's steps and soothe his
    thoughts.

"LYRE! THOUGH SUCH POWER DO IN THY MAGIC LIVE"

1842(?)   1842

LYRE! though such power do in thy magic live
   As might from India's farthest plain
   Recall the not unwilling Maid,
      Assist me to detain
      The lovely Fugitive:
Check with thy notes the impulse which, betrayed
By her sweet farewell looks, I longed to aid.
Here let me gaze enrapt upon that eye,
The impregnable and awe-inspiring fort
Of contemplation, the calm port
By reason fenced from winds that sigh
Among the restless sails of vanity.
But if no wish be hers that we should part,
A humbler bliss would satisfy my heart.
     Where all things are so fair,
Enough by her dear side to breathe the air
    Of this Elysian weather;
And, on or in, or near, the brook, espy
   Shade upon the sunshine lying
      Faint and somewhat pensively;

[192]

LYRE! THOUGH SUCH POWER

And downward Image gaily vying
      With its upright living tree
'Mid silver clouds, and openings of blue sky
As soft almost and deep as her cerulean eye.

Nor less the joy with many a glance
Cast up the Stream or down at her beseeching,
To mark its eddying foam-balls prettily distrest
By ever-changing shape and want of rest;
      Or watch, with mutual teaching,
      The current as it plays
      In flashing leaps and stealthy creeps
      Adown a rocky maze;
Or note (translucent summer's happiest chance!)
In the slope-channel floored with pebbles bright,
Stones of all hues, gem emulous of gem,
So vivid that they take from keenest sight
The liquid veil that seeks not to hide them.

TO THE CLOUDS

1842(?) 1842

These verses were suggested while I was walking on the
foot-road between Rydal Mount and Grasmere. The clouds
were driving over the top of Nab-Scar across the vale: they set
my thoughts agoing, and the rest followed almost immediately.

ARMY of Clouds! ye wingèd Hosts in troops
Ascending from behind the motionless brow
Of that tall rock, as from a hidden world,
Oh whither with such eagerness of speed?
What seek ye, or what shun ye? of the gale
Companions, fear ye to be left behind,
Or racing o'er your blue ethereal field
Contend ye with each other? of the sea
Children, thus post ye over vale and height
To sink upon your mother's lap — and rest?
Or were ye rightlier hailed, when first mine eyes
Beheld in your impetuous march the likeness
Of a wide army pressing on to meet
Or overtake some unknown enemy? —
But your smooth motions suit a peaceful aim;
And Fancy, not less aptly pleased, compares
Your squadrons to an endless flight of birds
Aërial, upon due migration bound

[194]

TO THE CLOUDS

To milder climes; or rather do ye urge
In caravan your hasty pilgrimage
To pause at last on more aspiring heights
Than these, and utter your devotion there
With thunderous voice? Or are ye jubilant,
And would ye, tracking your proud lord the Sun,
Be present at his setting; or the pomp
Of Persian mornings would ye fill, and stand
Poising your splendours high above the heads
Of worshippers kneeling to their up-risen God?
Whence, whence, ye Clouds! this eagerness of speed?
Speak, silent creatures. — They are gone, are fled,
Buried together in yon gloomy mass
That loads the middle heaven; and clear and bright
And vacant doth the region which they thronged
Appear; a calm descent of sky conducting
Down to the unapproachable abyss,
Down to that hidden gulf from which they rose
To vanish — fleet as days and months and years,
Fleet as the generations of mankind,
Power, glory, empire, as the world itself,
The lingering world, when time hath ceased to be.
But the winds roar, shaking the rooted trees,
And see! a bright precursor to a train
Perchance as numerous, overpeers the rock
That sullenly refuses to partake

Of the wild impulse. From a fount of life
Invisible, the long procession moves
Luminous or gloomy, welcome to the vale
Which they are entering, welcome to mine eye
That sees them, to my soul that owns in them,
And in the bosom of the firmament
O'er which they move, wherein they are contained,
A type of her capacious self and all
Her restless progeny.
                              A humble walk
Here is my body doomed to tread, this path,
A little hoary line and faintly traced,
Work, shall we call it, of the shepherd's foot
Or of his flock? — joint vestige of them both.
I pace it unrepining, for my thoughts
Admit no bondage and my words have wings.
Where is the Orphean lyre, or Druid harp,
To accompany the verse? The mountain blast
Shall be our *hand* of music; he shall sweep
The rocks, and quivering trees, and billowy lake,
And search the fibres of the caves, and they
Shall answer, for our song is of the Clouds.
And the wind loves them; and the gentle gales —
Which by their aid re-clothe the naked lawn
With annual verdure, and revive the woods,
And moisten the parched lips of thirsty flowers —

TO THE CLOUDS

Love them; and every idle breeze of air
Bends to the favourite burthen. Moon and stars
Keep their most solemn vigils when the Clouds
Watch also, shifting peaceably their place
Like bands of ministering Spirits, or when they lie,
As if some Protean art the change had wrought,
In listless quiet o'er the ethereal deep
Scattered, a Cyclades of various shapes
And all degrees of beauty. O ye Lightnings!
Ye are their perilous offspring; and the Sun —
Source inexhaustible of life and joy,
And type of man's far-darting reason, therefore
In old time worshipped as the god of verse,
A blazing intellectual deity —
Loves his own glory in their looks, and showers
Upon that unsubstantial brotherhood
Visions with all but beatific light
Enriched — too transient were they not renewed
From age to age, and did not, while we gaze
In silent rapture, credulous desire
Nourish the hope that memory lacks not power
To keep the treasure unimpaired. Vain thought!
Yet why repine, created as we are
For joy and rest, albeit to find them only
Lodged in the bosom of eternal things?

"WANSFELL! [19] THIS HOUSEHOLD HAS A FAVOURED LOT"

1842   1845

WANSFELL! this Household has a favoured lot,
Living with liberty on thee to gaze,
To watch while Morn first crowns thee with her rays,
Or when along thy breast serenely float
Evening's angelic clouds. Yet ne'er a note
Hath sounded (shame upon the Bard!) thy praise
For all that thou, as if from heaven, hast brought
Of glory lavished on our quiet days.
Bountiful Son of Earth! when we are gone
From every object dear to mortal sight,
As soon we shall be, may these words attest
How oft, to elevate our spirits, shone
Thy visionary majesties of light,
How in thy pensive glooms our hearts found rest.

THE EAGLE AND THE DOVE

1842   1842

SHADE of Caractacus, if spirits love
The cause they fought for in their earthly home
To see the Eagle ruffled by the Dove
May soothe thy memory of the chains of Rome.

These children claim thee for their sire; the breath
Of thy renown, from Cambrian mountains, fans
A flame within them that despises death
And glorifies the truant youth of Vannes.

With thy own scorn of tyrants they advance,
But truth divine has sanctified their rage,
A silver cross enchased with flowers of France
Their badge, attests the holy fight they wage.

The shrill defiance of the young crusade
Their veteran foes mock as an idle noise;
But unto Faith and Loyalty comes aid
From Heaven, gigantic force to beardless boys.

GRACE DARLING

1843 1845

AMONG the dwellers in the silent fields
The natural heart is touched, and public way
And crowded street resound with ballad strains,
Inspired by ONE whose very name bespeaks
Favour divine, exalting human love;
Whom, since her birth on bleak Northumbria's coast,
Known unto few but prized as far as known,
A single Act endears to high and low
Through the whole land — to Manhood, moved in spite
Of the world's freezing cares — to generous Youth —
To Infancy, that lisps her praise — to Age
Whose eye reflects it, glistening through a tear
Of tremulous admiration. Such true fame
Awaits her *now;* but, verily, good deeds
Do not imperishable record find
Save in the rolls of heaven, where hers may live
A theme for angels, when they celebrate
The high-souled virtues which forgetful earth
Has witnessed. Oh! that winds and waves could speak
Of things which their united power called forth
From the pure depths of her humanity!

GRACE DARLING

A Maiden gentle, yet, at duty's call,
Firm and unflinching, as the Lighthouse reared
On the Island-rock, her lonely dwelling-place;
Or like the invincible Rock itself that braves,
Age after age, the hostile elements,
As when it guarded holy Cuthbert's cell.

All night the storm had raged, nor ceased, nor paused,
When, as day broke, the Maid, through misty air,
Espies far off a Wreck, amid the surf,
Beating on one of those disastrous isles —
Half of a Vessel, half — no more; the rest
Had vanished, swallowed up with all that there
Had for the common safety striven in vain,
Or thither thronged for refuge. With quick glance
Daughter and Sire through optic-glass discern,
Clinging about the remnant of this Ship,
Creatures — how precious in the Maiden's sight!
For whom, belike, the old Man grieves still more
Than for their fellow-sufferers engulfed
Where every parting agony is hushed,
And hope and fear mix not in further strife.
"But courage, Father! let us out to sea —
A few may yet be saved." The Daughter's words,
Her earnest tone, and look beaming with faith,
Dispel the Father's doubts: nor do they lack
The noble-minded Mother's helping hand

GRACE DARLING

To launch the boat; and with her blessing cheered,
And inwardly sustained by silent prayer,
Together they put forth, Father and Child!
Each grasps an oar, and struggling on they go —
Rivals in effort; and, alike intent
Here to elude and there surmount, they watch
The billows lengthening, mutually crossed
And shattered, and re-gathering their might;
As if the tumult, by the Almighty's will
Were, in the conscious sea, roused and prolonged
That woman's fortitude — so tried, so proved —
May brighten more and more!
                              True to the mark,
They stem the current of that perilous gorge,
Their arms still strengthening with the strengthening
        heart,
Though danger, as the Wreck is neared, becomes
More imminent. Not unseen do they approach;
And rapture, with varieties of fear
Incessantly conflicting, thrills the frames
Of those who, in that dauntless energy,
Foretaste deliverance; but the least perturbed
Can scarcely trust his eyes, when he perceives
That of the pair — tossed on the waves to bring
Hope to the hopeless, to the dying, life —
One is a Woman, a poor earthly sister,

GRACE DARLING

Or, be the Visitant other than she seems,
A guardian Spirit sent from pitying Heaven,
In woman's shape. But why prolong the tale,
Casting weak words amid a host of thoughts
Armed to repel them? Every hazard faced
And difficulty mastered, with resolve
That no one breathing should be left to perish,
This last remainder of the crew are all
Placed in the little boat, then o'er the deep
Are safely borne, landed upon the beach,
And, in fulfilment of God's mercy, lodged
Within the sheltering Lighthouse. — Shout, ye Waves,
Send forth a song of triumph. Waves and Winds,
Exult in this deliverance wrought through faith
In Him whose Providence your rage hath served!
Ye screaming Sea-mews, in the concert join!
And would that some immortal Voice — a Voice
Fitly attuned to all that gratitude
Breathes out from floor or couch, through pallid lips
Of the survivors — to the clouds might bear —
Blended with praise of that parental love,
Beneath whose watchful eye the Maiden grew
Pious and pure, modest and yet so brave,
Though young so wise, though meek so resolute —
Might carry to the clouds and to the stars,
Yea, to celestial Choirs, GRACE DARLING's name!

"WHILE BEAMS OF ORIENT LIGHT SHOOT WIDE AND HIGH"

1843   1845

WHILE beams of orient light shoot wide and high,
Deep in the vale a little rural Town [20]
Breathes forth a cloud-like creature of its own,
That mounts not toward the radiant morning sky,
But, with a less ambitious sympathy,
Hangs o'er its Parent waking to the cares
Troubles and toils that every day prepares.
So Fancy, to the musing Poet's eye,
Endears that Lingerer. And how blest her sway
(Like influence never may my soul reject)
If the calm Heaven, now to its zenith decked
With glorious forms in numberless array,
To the lone shepherd on the hills disclose
Gleams from a world in which the saints repose.

TO THE REV. CHRISTOPHER WORDS-WORTH, D. D., MASTER OF HARROW SCHOOL

AFTER THE PERUSAL OF HIS "THEOPHILUS ANGLICA-NUS," RECENTLY PUBLISHED

1843   1845

ENLIGHTENED Teacher, gladly from thy hand
Have I received this proof of pains bestowed
By Thee to guide thy Pupils on the road
That, in our native isle, and every land,
The Church, when trusting in divine command
And in her Catholic attributes, hath trod:
O may these lessons be with profit scanned
To thy heart's wish, thy labour blest by God!
So the bright faces of the young and gay
Shall look more bright — the happy, happier still;
Catch, in the pauses of their keenest play,
Motions of thought which elevate the will
And, like the Spire that from your classic Hill
Points heavenward, indicate the end and way.

INSCRIPTION

FOR A MONUMENT IN CROSTHWAITE CHURCH, IN THE
VALE OF KESWICK

1843   1845

YE vales and hills whose beauty hither drew
The poet's steps, and fixed him here, on you
His eyes have closed! And ye, loved books, no more
Shall Southey feed upon your precious lore,
To works that ne'er shall forfeit their renown,
Adding immortal labours of his own —
Whether he traced historic truth, with zeal
For the State's guidance, or the Church's weal,
Or Fancy, disciplined by studious art,
Informed his pen, or wisdom of the heart,
Or judgments sanctioned in the Patriot's mind
By reverence for the rights of all mankind.
Wide were his aims, yet in no human breast
Could private feelings meet for holier rest.
His joys, his griefs, have vanished like a cloud
From Skiddaw's top; but he to heaven was vowed
Through his industrious life, and Christian faith
Calmed in his soul the fear of change and death.

ON THE PROJECTED KENDAL AND WINDERMERE RAILWAY [21]

1844   1845

Is then no nook of English ground secure
From rash assault? Schemes of retirement sown
In youth, and 'mid the busy world kept pure
As when their earliest flowers of hope were blown,
Must perish; — how can they this blight endure?
And must he too the ruthless change bemoan
Who scorns a false utilitarian lure
'Mid his paternal fields at random thrown?
Baffle the threat, bright Scene, from Orresthead
Given to the pausing traveller's rapturous glance:
Plead for thy peace, thou beautiful romance
Of nature; and, if human hearts be dead,
Speak, passing winds; ye torrents, with your strong
And constant voice, protest against the wrong.

"PROUD WERE YE, MOUNTAINS, WHEN, IN TIMES OF OLD"

1844 1845

PROUD were ye, Mountains, when, in times of old,
Your patriot sons, to stem invasive war,
Intrenched your brows; ye gloried in each scar:
Now, for your shame, a Power, the Thirst of Gold,
That rules o'er Britain like a baneful star,
Wills that your peace, your beauty, shall be sold,
And clear way made for her triumphal car
Through the beloved retreats your arms enfold!
Heard YE that Whistle? As her long-linked Train
Swept onwards, did the vision cross your view?
Yes, ye were startled; — and, in balance true,
Weighing the mischief with the promised gain,
Mountains, and Vales, and Floods, I call on you
To share the passion of a just disdain.

AT FURNESS ABBEY

1844   1845

HERE, where, of havoc tired and rash undoing,
Man left this Structure to become Time's prey
A soothing spirit follows in the way
That Nature takes, her counter-work pursuing,
See how her Ivy clasps the sacred Ruin
Fall to prevent or beautify decay;
And, on the mouldered walls, how bright, how gay,
The flowers in pearly dews their bloom renewing!
Thanks to the place, blessings upon the hour;
Even as I speak the rising Sun's first smile
Gleams on the grass-crowned top of yon tall Tower
Whose cawing occupants with joy proclaim
Prescriptive title to the shattered pile
Where, Cavendish, *thine* seems nothing but a name!

"FORTH FROM A JUTTING RIDGE, AROUND WHOSE BASE"

1845   1845

FORTH from a jutting ridge, around whose base
Winds our deep Vale, two heath-clad Rocks ascend
In fellowship, the loftiest of the pair
Rising to no ambitious height; yet both,
O'er lake and stream, mountain and flowery mead,
Unfolding prospects fair as human eyes
Ever beheld. Up-led with mutual help,
To one or other brow of those twin Peaks
Were two adventurous Sisters wont to climb,
And took no note of the hour while thence they gazed,
The blooming heath their couch, gazed, side by side,
In speechless admiration. I, a witness
And frequent sharer of their calm delight
With thankful heart, to either Eminence
Gave the baptismal name each Sister bore.
Now are they parted, far as Death's cold hand
Hath power to part the Spirits of those who love
As they did love. Ye kindred Pinnacles —
That, while the generations of mankind
Follow each other to their hiding-place

FORTH FROM A JUTTING RIDGE

In time's abyss, are privileged to endure
Beautiful in yourselves, and richly graced
With like command of beauty — grant your aid
For MARY's humble, SARAH's silent claim,
That their pure joy in nature may survive
From age to age in blended memory.

THE WESTMORELAND GIRL

TO MY GRANDCHILDREN

1845   1845

PART I

SEEK who will delight in fable
I shall tell you truth.   A Lamb
Leapt from this steep bank to follow
'Cross the brook its thoughtless dam.

Far and wide on hill and valley
Rain had fallen, unceasing rain,
And the bleating mother's Young-one
Struggled with the flood in vain:

But, as chanced, a Cottage-maiden
(Ten years scarcely had she told)
Seeing, plunged into the torrent,
Clasped the Lamb and kept her hold.

Whirled adown the rocky channel,
Sinking, rising, on they go,
Peace and rest, as seems, before them
Only in the lake below.

[212]

THE WESTMORELAND GIRL

Oh! it was a frightful current
Whose fierce wrath the Girl had braved;
Clap your hands with joy my Hearers,
Shout in triumph, both are saved;

Saved by courage that with danger
Grew, by strength the gift of love,
And belike a guardian angel
Came with succour from above.

PART II

Now, to a maturer Audience,
Let me speak of this brave Child
Left among her native mountains
With wild Nature to run wild.

So, unwatched by love maternal,
Mother's care no more her guide,
Fared this little bright-eyed Orphan
Even while at her father's side.

Spare your blame, — remembrance makes him
Loth to rule by strict command;
Still upon his cheek are living
Touches of her infant hand,

Dear caresses given in pity,
Sympathy that soothed his grief,

[213]

As the dying mother witnessed
To her thankful mind's relief.

Time passed on; the Child was happy,
Like a Spirit of air she moved,
Wayward, yet by all who knew her
For her tender heart beloved.

Scarcely less than sacred passions,
Bred in house, in grove, and field,
Link her with the inferior creatures,
Urge her powers their rights to shield.

Anglers, bent on reckless pastime,
Learn how she can feel alike
Both for tiny harmless minnow
And the fierce and sharp-toothed pike.

Merciful protectress, kindling
Into anger or disdain;
Many a captive hath she rescued,
Others saved from lingering pain.

Listen yet awhile; — with patience
Hear the homely truths I tell,
She in Grasmere's old church-steeple
Tolled this day the passing-bell.

THE WESTMORELAND GIRL

Yes, the wild Girl of the mountains
To their echoes gave the sound,
Notice punctual as the minute,
Warning solemn and profound.

She, fulfilling her sire's office,
Rang alone the far-heard knell,
Tribute, by her hand, in sorrow,
Paid to One who loved her well.

When his spirit was departed
On that service she went forth;
Nor will fail the like to render
When his corse is laid in earth.

What then wants the Child to temper,
In her breast, unruly fire,
To control the froward impulse
And restrain the vague desire?

Easily a pious training
And a stedfast outward power
Would supplant the weeds and cherish,
In their stead, each opening flower.

Thus the fearless Lamb-deliv'rer,
Woman-grown, meek-hearted, sage,

May become a blest example
For her sex, of every age.

Watchful as a wheeling eagle,
Constant as a soaring lark,
Should the country need a heroine,
She might prove our Maid of Arc.

Leave that thought; and here be uttered
Prayer that Grace divine may raise
Her humane courageous spirit
Up to heaven, thro' peaceful ways.

AT FURNESS ABBEY

1845   1845

WELL have yon Railway Labourers to THIS ground
Withdrawn for noontide rest. They sit, they walk
Among the Ruins, but no idle talk
Is heard; to grave demeanour all are bound;
And from one voice a Hymn with tuneful sound
Hallows once more the long-deserted Quire
And thrills the old sepulchral earth, around.
Others look up, and with fixed eyes admire
That wide-spanned arch, wondering how it was raised,
To keep, so high in air, its strength and grace:
All seem to feel the spirit of the place,
And by the general reverence God is praised:
Profane Despoilers, stand ye not reproved,
While thus these simple-hearted men are moved?

"YES! THOU ART FAIR, YET BE NOT MOVED"

1845   1845

YES! thou art fair, yet be not moved
  To scorn the declaration,
That sometimes I in thee have loved
  My fancy's own creation.

Imagination needs must stir;
  Dear Maid, this truth believe,
Minds that have nothing to confer
  Find little to perceive.

Be pleased that nature made thee fit
  To feed my heart's devotion,
By laws to which all Forms submit
  In sky, air, earth, and ocean.

"WHAT HEAVENLY SMILES! O LADY MINE"

1845   1845

WHAT heavenly smiles! O Lady mine
Through my very heart they shine;
And, if my brow gives back their light,
Do thou look gladly on the sight;
As the clear Moon with modest pride
  Beholds her own bright beams
Reflected from the mountain's side
  And from the headlong streams.

TO A LADY

IN ANSWER TO A REQUEST THAT I WOULD WRITE HER A
POEM UPON SOME DRAWINGS THAT SHE HAD MADE OF
FLOWERS IN THE ISLAND OF MADEIRA

1845   1845

FAIR Lady! can I sing of flowers
  That in Madeira bloom and fade,
I who ne'er sate within their bowers,
  Nor through their sunny lawns have strayed?
How they in sprightly dance are worn
  By Shepherd-groom or May-day queen,
Or holy festal pomps adorn,
  These eyes have never seen.

Yet tho' to me the pencil's art
  No like remembrances can give,
Your portraits still may reach the heart
  And there for gentle pleasure live;
While Fancy ranging with free scope
  Shall on some lovely Alien set
A name with us endeared to hope,
  To peace, or fond regret.

TO A LADY

Still as we look with nicer care,
　Some new resemblance we may trace:
A *Heart's-ease* will perhaps be there,
　A *Speedwell* may not want its place.
And so may we, with charmèd mind
　Beholding what your skill has wrought,
Another *Star-of-Bethlehem* find,
　A new *Forget-me-not.*

From earth to heaven with motion fleet
　From heaven to earth our thoughts will pass,
A *Holy-thistle* here we meet
　And there a *Shepherd's weather-glass;*
And haply some familiar name
　Shall grace the fairest, sweetest plant
Whose presence cheers the drooping frame
　Of English Emigrant.

Gazing she feels its powers beguile
　Sad thoughts, and breathes with easier breath;
Alas! that meek, that tender smile
　Is but a harbinger of death:
And pointing with a feeble hand
　She says, in faint words by sighs broken,
Bear for me to my native land
　This precious Flower, true love's last token.

"GLAD SIGHT WHEREVER NEW WITH OLD"

1845(?) 1845

GLAD sight wherever new with old
Is joined through some dear homeborn tie;
The life of all that we behold
Depends upon that mystery.
Vain is the glory of the sky,
The beauty vain of field and grove,
Unless, while with admiring eye
We gaze, we also learn to love.

LOVE LIES BLEEDING

1845(?)   1845

It has been said that the English, though their country has produced so many great poets, is now the most unpoetical nation in Europe. It is probably true; for they have more temptation to become so than any other European people. Trade, commerce, and manufactures, physical science, and mechanic arts, out of which so much wealth has arisen, have made our countrymen infinitely less sensible to movements of imagination and fancy than were our forefathers in their simple state of society. How touching and beautiful were, in most instances, the names they gave to our indigenous flowers, or any other they were familiarly acquainted with! — Every month for many years have we been importing plants and flowers from all quarters of the globe, many of which are spread through our gardens, and some perhaps likely to be met with on the few Commons which we have left. Will their botanical names ever be displaced by plain English appellations, which will bring them home to our hearts by connection with our joys and sorrows? It can never be, unless society treads back her steps towards those simplicities which have been banished by the undue influence of towns spreading and spreading in every direction, so that city-life with every generation takes more and more the lead of rural. Among the ancients, villages were reckoned the seats of barbarism. Refinement, for the most part false, increases the desire to accumulate wealth; and while theories of political economy are boastfully pleading for the practice, inhumanity pervades all our dealings in buying and selling. This selfishness wars against disinterested imagination in all directions, and, evils coming round in a circle, barbarism spreads in every quarter of our island. Oh for the reign of justice, and then the humblest man among us would have more power and dignity in and about him than the highest have now!

You call it, "Love lies bleeding," — so you may,
Though the red Flower, not prostrate, only droops,
As we have seen it here from day to day,
From month to month, life passing not away:
A flower how rich in sadness! Even thus stoops,
(Sentient by Grecian sculpture's marvellous power)
Thus leans, with hanging brow and body bent
Earthward in uncomplaining languishment
The dying Gladiator. So, sad Flower!
('T is Fancy guides me willing to be led,
Though by a slender thread)
So drooped Adonis bathed in sanguine dew
Of his death-wound, when he from innocent air
The gentlest breath of resignation drew;
While Venus in a passion of despair
Rent, weeping over him, her golden hair,
Spangled with drops of that celestial shower.
She suffered, as Immortals sometimes do;
But pangs more lasting far, *that* Lover knew
Who first, weighed down by scorn, in some lone
     tower

LOVE LIES BLEEDING

Did press this semblance of unpitied smart
Into the service of his constant heart,
His own dejection, downcast Flower! could share
With thine, and gave the mournful name which thou
    wilt ever bear.

COMPANION TO THE FOREGOING

1845(?)   1845

NEVER enlivened with the liveliest ray
That fosters growth or checks or cheers decay,
Nor by the heaviest rain-drops more deprest,
This Flower, that first appeared as summer's guest,
Preserves her beauty 'mid autumnal leaves
And to her mournful habits fondly cleaves.
When files of stateliest plants have ceased to bloom,
One after one submitting to their doom,
When her coevals each and all are fled,
What keeps her thus reclined upon her lonesome bed?
  The old mythologists, more impressed than we
Of this late day by character in tree
Or herb, that claimed peculiar sympathy,
Or by the silent lapse of fountain clear,
Or with the language of the viewless air
By bird or beast made vocal, sought a cause
To solve the mystery, not in Nature's laws
But in Man's fortunes. Hence a thousand tales
Sung to the plaintive lyre in Grecian vales.
Nor doubt that something of their spirit swayed
The fancy-stricken Youth or heart-sick Maid,

COMPANION TO THE FOREGOING

Who, while each stood companionless and eyed
This undeparting Flower of crimson dyed,
Thought of a wound which death is slow to cure,
A fate that has endured and will endure,
And, patience coveting yet passion feeding,
Called the dejected Lingerer, *Loves lies bleeding.*

THE CUCKOO–CLOCK

1845   1845

Of this clock I have nothing further to say than what the
poem expresses, except that it must be here recorded that it
was a present from the dear friend for whose sake these notes
were chiefly undertaken, and who has written them from my
dictation.

WOULDST thou be taught, when sleep has taken flight,
By a sure voice that can most sweetly tell,
How far off yet a glimpse of morning light,
And if to lure the truant back be well,
Forbear to covet a Repeater's stroke,
That, answering to thy touch, will sound the hour;
Better provide thee with a Cuckoo-clock
For service hung behind thy chamber-door;
And in due time the soft spontaneous shock,
The double note, as if with living power,
Will to composure lead — or make thee blithe as bird
    in bower.

List, Cuckoo — Cuckoo! — oft tho' tempests howl,
Or nipping frost remind thee trees are bare,
How cattle pine, and droop the shivering fowl,
Thy spirits will seem to feed on balmy air;

THE CUCKOO-CLOCK

I speak with knowledge, — by that Voice beguiled,
Thou wilt salute old memories as they throng
Into thy heart; and fancies, running wild
Through fresh green fields, and budding groves among,
Will make thee happy, happy as a child:
Of sunshine wilt thou think, and flowers, and song,
And breathe as in a world where nothing can go wrong.

And know — that, even for him who shuns the day
And nightly tosses on a bed of pain;
Whose joys, from all but memory swept away,
Must come unhoped for, if they come again;
Know — that, for him whose waking thoughts, severe
As his distress is sharp, would scorn my theme,
The mimic notes, striking upon his ear
In sleep, and intermingling with his dream,
Could from sad regions send him to a dear
Delightful land of verdure, shower and gleam,
To mock the *wandering* Voice beside some haunted
        stream.

O bounty without measure! while the grace
Of Heaven doth in such wise, from humblest springs,
Pour pleasure forth, and solaces that trace
A mazy course along familiar things,
Well may our hearts have faith that blessings come,

THE CUCKOO–CLOCK

Streaming from founts above the starry sky,
With angels when their own untroubled home
They leave, and speed on nightly embassy
To visit earthly chambers, — and for whom?
Yea, both for souls who God's forbearance try,
And those that seek his help, and for his mercy sigh.

"SO FAIR, SO SWEET, WITHAL SO SENSITIVE"

1845   1845

So fair, so sweet, withal so sensitive,
Would that the little Flowers were born to live,
Conscious of half the pleasure which they give;

That to this mountain-daisy's self were known
The beauty of its star-shaped shadow, thrown
On the smooth surface of this naked stone!

And what if hence a bold desire should mount
High as the Sun, that he could take account
Of all that issues from his glorious fount!

So might he ken how by his sovereign aid
These delicate companionships are made;
And how he rules the pomp of light and shade;

And were the Sister-power that shines by night
So privileged, what a countenance of delight
Would through the clouds break forth on human
      sight!

SO FAR, SO SWEET

Fond fancies! wheresoe'er shall turn thine eye
On earth, air, ocean, or the starry sky,
Converse with Nature in pure sympathy;

All vain desires, all lawless wishes quelled,
Be Thou to love and praise alike impelled,
Whatever boon is granted or withheld.

TO THE PENNSYLVANIANS

1845 1845

Days undefiled by luxury or sloth,
Firm self-denial, manners grave and staid,
Rights equal, laws with cheerfulness obeyed,
Words that require no sanction from an oath,
And simple honesty a common growth —
This high repute, with bounteous Nature's aid,
Won confidence, now ruthlessly betrayed
At will, your power the measure of your troth! —
All who revere the memory of Penn
Grieve for the land on whose wild woods his name
Was fondly grafted with a virtuous aim,
Renounced, abandoned by degenerate Men
For state-dishonour black as ever came
To upper air from Mammon's loathsome den.

"YOUNG ENGLAND — WHAT IS THEN BECOME OF OLD"

1845   1845

YOUNG ENGLAND — What is then become of Old,
Of dear Old England? Think they she is dead,
Dead to the very name? Presumption fed
On empty air! That name will keep its hold
In the true filial bosom's inmost fold
For ever. — The Spirit of Alfred, at the head
Of all who for her rights watched, toiled and bled,
Knows that this prophecy is not too bold.
What — how! shall she submit in will and deed
To Beardless Boys — an imitative race,
The *servum pecus* of a Gallic breed?
Dear Mother! if thou *must* thy steps retrace,
Go where at least meek innocency dwells;
Let Babes and Sucklings be thy oracles.

"THOUGH THE BOLD WINGS OF POESY AFFECT"

1845(?)   1845

THOUGH the bold wings of Poesy affect
The clouds, and wheel around the mountain tops
Rejoicing, from her loftiest height she drops
Well pleased to skim the plain with wild flowers deckt
Or muse in solemn grove whose shades protect
The lingering dew — there steals along, or stops
Watching the least small bird that round her hops,
Or creeping worm, with sensitive respect.
Her functions are they therefore less divine,
Her thoughts less deep, or void of grave intent
Her simplest fancies? Should that fear be thine,
Aspiring Votary, ere thy hand present
One offering, kneel before her modest shrine,
With brow in penitential sorrow bent!

SUGGESTED BY A PICTURE OF THE BIRD OF PARADISE

1845(?) 1845

This subject has been treated of in another note. I will here only by way of comment direct attention to the fact that pictures of animals and other productions of nature as seen in conservatories, menageries, museums, etc., would do little for the national mind, nay they would be rather injurious to it, if the imagination were excluded by the presence of the object, more or less out of a state of nature. If it were not that we learn to talk and think of the lion and the eagle, the palm-tree and even the cedar, from the impassioned introduction of them so frequently into Holy Scripture and by great poets, and divines who write as poets, the spiritual part of our nature, and therefore the higher part of it, would derive no benefit from such intercourse with such objects.

THE gentlest Poet, with free thoughts endowed,
And a true master of the glowing strain,
Might scan the narrow province with disdain
That to the Painter's skill is here allowed.
This, this the Bird of Paradise! disclaim
The daring thought, forget the name;
This the Sun's Bird, whom Glendoveers might
      own
As no unworthy Partner in their flight

THE BIRD OF PARADISE

Through seas of ether, where the ruffling sway
Of nether air's rude billows is unknown;
Whom Sylphs, if e'er for casual pastime they
Through India's spicy regions wing their way,
Might bow to as their Lord. What character,
O sovereign Nature! I appeal to thee,
Of all thy feathered progeny
Is so unearthly, and what shape so fair?
So richly decked in variegated down,
Green, sable, shining yellow, shadowy brown,
Tints softly with each other blended,
Hues doubtfully begun and ended;
Or intershooting, and to sight
Lost and recovered, as the rays of light
Glance on the conscious plumes touched here
        and there?
Full surely, when with such proud gifts of life
Began the pencil's strife,
O'erweening Art was caught as in a snare.

A sense of seemingly presumptuous wrong
Gave the first impulse to the Poet's song;
But, of his scorn repenting soon, he drew
A juster judgment from a calmer view;
And, with a spirit freed from discontent,
Thankfully took an effort that was meant
Not with God's bounty, Nature's love to vie,

Or made with hope to please that inward eye
Which ever strives in vain itself to satisfy,
But to recall the truth by some faint trace
Of power ethereal and celestial grace,
That in the living Creature find on earth a place.

SONNET

1846   1850

WHY should we weep or mourn, Angelic boy,
For such thou wert ere from our sight removed,
Holy, and ever dutiful — beloved
From day to day with never-ceasing joy,
And hopes as dear as could the heart employ
In aught to earth pertaining? Death has proved
His might, nor less his mercy, as behoved —
Death conscious that he only could destroy
The bodily frame. That beauty is laid low
To moulder in a far-off field of Rome;
But Heaven is now, blest Child, thy Spirit's home:
When such divine communion, which we know,
Is felt, thy Roman burial place will be
Surely a sweet remembrancer of Thee.

"WHERE LIES THE TRUTH? HAS MAN, IN WISDOM'S CREED"

1846 1850

WHERE lies the truth? has Man, in wisdom's creed,
A pitiable doom; for respite brief
A care more anxious, or a heavier grief?
Is he ungrateful, and doth little heed
God's bounty, soon forgotten; or indeed,
Must Man, with labour born, awake to sorrow
When Flowers rejoice and Larks with rival speed
Spring from their nests to bid the Sun good morrow?
They mount for rapture as their songs proclaim
Warbled in hearing both of earth and sky;
But o'er the contrast wherefore heave a sigh?
Like those aspirants let us soar — our aim,
Through life's worst trials, whether shocks or snares,
A happier, brighter, purer Heaven than theirs.

"I KNOW AN AGED MAN CONSTRAINED TO DWELL"

1846   1850

I KNOW an aged Man constrained to dwell
In a large house of public charity,
Where he abides, as in a Prisoner's cell,
With numbers near, alas! no company.

When he could creep about, at will, though poor
And forced to live on alms, this old Man fed
A Redbreast, one that to his cottage door
Came not, but in a lane partook his bread.

There, at the root of one particular tree,
An easy seat this worn-out Labourer found
While Robin pecked the crumbs upon his knee
Laid one by one, or scattered on the ground.

Dear intercourse was theirs, day after day;
What signs of mutual gladness when they met!
Think of their common peace, their simple play,
The parting moment and its fond regret.

[241]

I KNOW AN AGED MAN

Months passed in love that failed not to fulfil,
In spite of season's change, its own demand,
By fluttering pinions here and busy bill;
There by caresses from a tremulous hand.

Thus in the chosen spot a tie so strong
Was formed between the solitary pair,
That when his fate had housed him 'mid a throng
The Captive shunned all converse proffered there.

Wife, children, kindred, they were dead and gone;
But, if no evil hap his wishes crossed,
One living Stay was left, and on that one
Some recompence for all that he had lost.

Oh that the good old Man had power to prove,
By message sent through air or visible token,
That still he loves the Bird, and still must love;
That friendship lasts though fellowship is broken!

"HOW BEAUTIFUL THE QUEEN OF NIGHT"

1846(?) 1850

How beautiful the Queen of Night, on high
Her way pursuing among scattered clouds,
Where, ever and anon, her head she shrouds
Hidden from view in dense obscurity.
But look, and to the watchful eye
A brightening edge will indicate that soon
We shall behold the struggling Moon
Break forth, — again to walk the clear blue sky.

EVENING VOLUNTARIES

TO LUCCA GIORDANO

1846   1850

GIORDANO, verily thy Pencil's skill
Hath here portrayed with Nature's happiest grace
The fair Endymion couched on Latmos-hill;
And Dian gazing on the Shepherd's face
In rapture, — yet suspending her embrace,
As not unconscious with what power the thrill
Of her most timid touch his sleep would chase,
And, with his sleep, that beauty calm and still.
Oh may this work have found its last retreat
Here in a Mountain-bard's secure abode,
One to whom, yet a School-boy, Cynthia showed
A face of love which he in love would greet,
Fixed, by her smile, upon some rocky seat;
Or lured along where greenwood paths he trod.

"WHO BUT IS PLEASED TO WATCH THE MOON ON HIGH"

1846   1850

Who but is pleased to watch the moon on high
Travelling where she from time to time enshrouds
Her head, and nothing loth her Majesty
Renounces, till among the scattered clouds
One with its kindling edge declares that soon
Will appear before the uplifted eye
A Form as bright, as beautiful a moon,
To glide in open prospect through clear sky.
Pity that such a promise e'er should prove
False in the issue, that yon seeming space
Of sky should be in truth the stedfast face
Of a cloud flat and dense, through which must move
(By transit not unlike man's frequent doom)
The Wanderer lost in more determined gloom.

ILLUSTRATED BOOKS AND NEWSPAPERS

1846   1850

DISCOURSE was deemed Man's noblest attribute,
And written words the glory of his hand;
Then followed Printing with enlarged command
For thought — dominion vast and absolute
For spreading truth, and making love expand.
Now prose and verse sunk into disrepute
Must lacquey a dumb Art that best can suit
The taste of this once-intellectual Land.
A backward movement surely have we here,
From manhood, — back to childhood; for the age —
Back towards caverned life's first rude career.
Avaunt this vile abuse of pictured page!
Must eyes be all in all, the tongue and ear
Nothing? Heaven keep us from a lower stage!

"THE UNREMITTING VOICE OF NIGHTLY STREAMS"

1846   1850

THE unremitting voice of nightly streams
That wastes so oft, we think, its tuneful powers,
If neither soothing to the worm that gleams
Through dewy grass, nor small birds hushed in
      bowers,
Nor unto silent leaves and drowsy flowers, —
That voice of unpretending harmony
(For who what is shall measure by what seems
To be, or not to be,
Or tax high Heaven with prodigality?)
Wants not a healing influence that can creep
Into the human breast, and mix with sleep
To regulate the motion of our dreams
For kindly issues — as through every clime
Was felt near murmuring brooks in earliest time;
As at this day, the rudest swains who dwell
Where torrents roar, or hear the tinkling knell
Of water-breaks, with grateful heart could tell.

SONNET

TO AN OCTOGENARIAN

1846   1850

AFFECTIONS lose their object; Time brings forth
No successors; and, lodged in memory,
If love exists no longer, it must die, —
Wanting accustomed food, must pass from earth,
Or never hope to reach a second birth.
This sad belief, the happiest that is left
To thousands, share not Thou; howe'er bereft,
Scorned, or neglected, fear not such a dearth.
Though poor and destitute of friends thou art,
Perhaps the sole survivor of thy race,
One to whom Heaven assigns that mournful part
The utmost solitude of age to face,
Still shall be left some corner of the heart
Where Love for living Thing can find a place.

The Rocky Stream

ON THE BANKS OF A ROCKY STREAM

1846   1849

BEHOLD an emblem of our human mind
Crowded with thoughts that need a settled home,
Yet, like to eddying balls of foam
Within this whirlpool, they each other chase
Round and round, and neither find
An outlet nor a resting-place!
Stranger, if such disquietude be thine,
Fall on thy knees and sue for help divine.

ODE ON THE INSTALLATION OF HIS ROYAL HIGHNESS PRINCE ALBERT AS CHANCELLOR OF THE UNIVERSITY OF CAMBRIDGE, JULY 1847

1847   1847

INTRODUCTION AND CHORUS

For thirst of power that Heaven disowns,
For temples, towers, and thrones,
Too long insulted by the Spoiler's shock,
Indignant Europe cast
Her stormy foe at last
To reap the whirlwind on a Libyan rock.

SOLO — (TENOR)

War is passion's basest game
Madly played to win a name;
Up starts some tyrant, Earth and Heaven to dare,
The servile million bow;
But will the lightning glance aside to spare
The Despot's laurelled brow?

[250]

ODE

CHORUS

War is mercy, glory, fame,
Waged in Freedom's holy cause;
Freedom, such as Man may claim
Under God's restraining laws.
Such is Albion's fame and glory:
Let rescued Europe tell the story.

RECIT. (*accompanied*) — (CONTRALTO)

But lo, what sudden cloud has darkened all
    The land as with a funeral pall?
The Rose of England suffers blight,
The flower has drooped, the Isle's delight,
    Flower and bud together fall —
A Nation's hopes lie crushed in Claremont's
    desolate hall.

AIR — (SOPRANO)

Time a chequered mantle wears; —
    Earth awakes from wintry sleep;
Again the Tree a blossom bears —
    Cease, Britannia, cease to weep!
Hark to the peals on this bright May morn!
They tell that your future Queen is born.

ODE

SOPRANO SOLO AND CHORUS

A Guardian Angel fluttered
Above the Babe, unseen;
One word he softly uttered —
It named the future Queen:
And a joyful cry through the Island rang,
As clear and bold as the trumpet's clang,
As bland as the reed of peace —
"VICTORIA be her name!"
For righteous triumphs are the base
Whereon Britannia rests her peaceful fame.

QUARTET

Time, in his mantle's sunniest fold,
Uplifted in his arms the child;
And, while the fearless Infant smiled,
Her happier destiny foretold: —
"Infancy, by Wisdom mild,
  Trained to health and artless beauty;
Youth, by pleasure unbeguiled
 From the lore of lofty duty;
Womanhood is pure renown,
Seated on her lineal throne:
Leaves of myrtle in her Crown,
Fresh with lustre all their own.

[252]

ODE

Love, the treasure worth possessing,
More than all the world beside,
This shall be her choicest blessing,
Oft to royal hearts denied."

RECIT. (accompanied) — (BASS)

That eve, the Star of Brunswick shone
    With stedfast ray benign
On Gotha's ducal roof, and on
    The softly flowing Leine;
Nor failed to gild the spires of Bonn,
    And glittered on the Rhine —
Old Camus, too, on that prophetic night
    Was conscious of the ray;
And his willows whispered in its light,
    Not to the Zephyr's sway,
But with a Delphic life, in sight
    Of this auspicious day:

CHORUS

This day, when Granta hails her chosen Lord,
  And proud of her award,
    Confiding in the Star serene,
Welcomes the Consort of a happy Queen.

[253]

ODE

AIR — (CONTRALTO)

Prince, in these Collegiate bowers,
Where Science, leagued with holier truth,
Guards the sacred heart of youth,
Solemn monitors are ours.
These reverend aisles, these hallowed towers,
Raised by many a hand august,
Are haunted by majestic Powers,
The memories of the Wise and Just,
Who, faithful to a pious trust,
Here, in the Founder's spirit sought
To mould and stamp the ore of thought
In that bold form and impress high
That best betoken patriot loyalty.
Not in vain those Sages taught, —
True disciples, good as great,
Have pondered here their country's weal,
Weighed the Future by the Past,
Learned how social frames may last,
And how a Land may rule its fate
By constancy inviolate,
Though worlds to their foundations reel
The sport of factious Hate or godless Zeal.

ODE

AIR — (BASS)

Albert, in thy race we cherish
A Nation's strength that will not perish
While England's sceptred Line
True to the King of Kings is found;
Like that Wise ancestor of thine
Who threw the Saxon shield o'er Luther's life,
When first above the yells of bigot strife
The trumpet of the Living Word
Assumed a voice of deep portentous sound,
From gladdened Elbe to startled Tiber heard.

CHORUS

What shield more sublime
E'er was blazoned or sung?
And the PRINCE whom we greet
From its Hero is sprung.
Resound, resound the strain,
That hails him for our own!
Again, again, and yet again,
For the Church, the State, the Throne!
And that Presence fair and bright,
Ever blest wherever seen,
Who deigns to grace our festal rite,
The pride of the Islands, VICTORIA THE QUEEN.

IN WORDSWORTH'S COUNTRY

BY

JOHN BURROUGHS

IN WORDSWORTH'S COUNTRY

BY

JOHN BURROUGHS

No other English poet had touched me quite so closely as Wordsworth. All cultivated men delight in Shakespeare; he is the universal genius; but Wordsworth's poetry has more the character of a message, and a message special and personal, to a comparatively small circle of readers. He stands for a particular phase of human thought and experience, and his service to certain minds is like an initiation into a new order of truths. Note what a revelation he was to the logical mind of John Stuart Mill. His limitations make him all the more private and precious, like the seclusion of one of his mountain dales. He is not and can never be the world's poet, but more especially the poet of those who love solitude and solitary communion with nature. Shakespeare's attitude toward nature is for the most part like that of a gay, careless reveler, who leaves his companions for a moment to pluck a flower or gather a shell here and there, as they stroll

> By pavèd fountain, or by rushy brook,
> Or on the beachèd margent of the sea.

He is, of course, preëminent in all purely poetic achievements, but his poems can never minister to the spirit in the way Wordsworth's do.

[259]

IN WORDSWORTH'S COUNTRY

One can hardly appreciate the extent to which the latter poet has absorbed and reproduced the spirit of the Westmoreland scenery until he has visited that region. I paused there a few days in early June, on my way south, and again on my return late in July. I walked up from Windermere to Grasmere, where, on the second visit, I took up my abode at the historic Swan Inn, where Scott used to go surreptitiously to get his mug of beer when he was stopping with Wordsworth.

The call of the cuckoo came to me from over Rydal Water as I passed along. I plucked my first foxglove by the roadside; paused and listened to the voice of the mountain torrent; heard

The cataracts blow their trumpets from the steep;

caught many a glimpse of green, unpeopled hills, urn-shaped dells, treeless heights, rocky promontories, secluded valleys, and clear, swift-running streams. The scenery was sombre; there were but two colors, green and brown, verging on black; wherever the rock cropped out of the green turf on the mountain-sides, or in the vale, it showed a dark face. But the tenderness and freshness of the green tints were something to remember, — the hue of the first springing April grass, massed and widespread in midsummer.

Then there was a quiet splendor, almost grandeur, about Grasmere vale, such as I had not seen elsewhere, — a kind of monumental beauty and dignity that agreed well with one's conception of the loftier strains of its

[260]

poet. It is not too much dominated by the mountains, though shut in on all sides by them; that stately level floor of the valley keeps them back and defines them, and they rise from its outer margin like rugged, green-tufted, and green-draped walls.

It is doubtless this feature, as De Quincey says, this floor-like character of the valley, that makes the scenery of Grasmere more impressive than the scenery in North Wales, where the physiognomy of the mountains is essentially the same, but where the valleys are more bowl-shaped. Amid so much that is steep and rugged and broken, the eye delights in the repose and equilibrium of horizontal lines, — a bit of table-land, the surface of the lake, or the level of the valley bottom. The principal valleys of our own Catskill region all have this stately floor, so characteristic of Wordsworth's country. It was a pleasure which I daily indulged in to stand on the bridge by Grasmere Church, with that full, limpid stream before me, pausing and deepening under the stone embankment near where the dust of the poet lies, and let the eye sweep across the plain to the foot of the near mountains, or dwell upon their encircling summits above the tops of the trees and the roofs of the village. The water-ouzel loved to linger there, too, and would sit in contemplative mood on the stones around which the water loitered and murmured, its clear white breast alone defining it from the object upon which it rested. Then it would trip along the margin of the pool, or flit a few feet over its surface, and suddenly, as if it had burst like a bubble, vanish before my eyes; there would be a little splash of the water beneath where I saw it, as if the drop of which it was composed had reunited with the surface there. Then, in a moment or two, it would emerge from the water and take up its stand as dry and unruffled as ever. It was always amusing to see this plump little bird, so unlike a water-fowl in shape and manner, disappear in the stream. It did not seem to dive, but simply dropped into the water, as if its wings had suddenly failed it. Sometimes it fairly tumbled in from its perch. It was gone from sight in a twinkling, and, while you were wondering how it could accomplish the feat of walking on the bottom of the stream under there, it reappeared as unconcerned as possible. It is a song-bird, a thrush, and gives a feature to these mountain streams and waterfalls which ours, except on the Pacific coast, entirely lack. The stream that winds through Grasmere vale, and flows against the embankment of the churchyard, as the Avon at Stratford, is of great beauty, — clean, bright, full, trouty, with just a tinge of gypsy blood in its veins, which it gets from the black tarns on the mountains, and which adds to its richness of color. I saw an angler take a few trout from it, in a meadow near the village. After a heavy rain the stream was not roily, but slightly darker in hue; these fields and mountains are so turf-bound that no particle of soil is carried away by the water.

Falls and cascades are a great feature all through this country, as they are a marked feature in Wordsworth's poetry. One's ear is everywhere haunted by the sound of falling water; and, when the ear cannot hear them, the eye can see the streaks or patches of white foam down the green declivities. There are no trees above the valley bottom to obstruct the view, and no hum of woods to muffle the sounds of distant streams. When I was at Grasmere there was much rain, and this stanza of the poet came to mind: —

> Loud is the Vale! The voice is up
> With which she speaks when storms are gone,
> A mighty unison of streams!
> Of all her voices, one!

The words "vale" and "dell" come to have a new meaning after one has visited Wordsworth's country, just as the words "cottage" and "shepherd" also have so much more significance there and in Scotland than at home.

> Dear Child of Nature, let them rail!
> — There is a nest in a green dale,
> A harbour and a hold,
> Where thou, a Wife and Friend, shalt see
> Thy own heart-stirring days, and be
> A light to young and old.

Every humble dwelling looks like a nest; that in which the poet himself lived had a cosy, nest-like look; and every vale is green, — a cradle amid rocky heights, padded and carpeted with the thickest turf.

Wordsworth is described as the poet of nature. He is more the poet of man, deeply wrought upon by a certain phase of nature, — the nature of those sombre, quiet, green, far-reaching mountain solitudes. There is a shepherd quality about him; he loves the flocks, the heights, the tarn, the tender herbage, the sheltered dell, the fold, with a kind of poetized shepherd instinct. Lambs and sheep and their haunts, and those who tend them, recur perpetually in his poems. How well his verse harmonizes with those high, green, and gray solitudes, where the silence is broken only by the bleat of lambs or sheep, or just stirred by the voice of distant waterfalls! Simple, elemental, yet profoundly tender and human, he had

> The primal sympathy
> Which, having been, must ever be.

He brooded upon nature, but it was nature mirrored in his own heart. In his poem of "The Brothers" he says of his hero, who had gone to sea: —

> He had been reared
> Among the mountains, and he in his heart
> Was half a shepherd on the stormy seas.
> Oft in the piping shrouds had Leonard heard
> The tones of waterfalls, and inland sounds
> Of caves and trees;

and, leaning over the vessel's side and gazing into the "broad blue wave and sparkling foam," he

> Saw mountains; saw the forms of sheep that grazed
> On verdant hills.

This was what his own heart told him; every experience or sentiment called those beloved images to his own mind.

One afternoon, when the sun seemed likely to get the better of the soft rain-clouds, I set out to climb to the top of Helvellyn. I followed the highway a mile or more beyond the Swan Inn, and then I committed myself to a footpath that turns up the mountain-side to the right, and crosses into Grisedale and so to Ulleswater. Two schoolgirls whom I overtook put me on the right track. The voice of a foaming mountain torrent was in my ears a long distance, and now and then the path crossed it. Fairfield Mountain was on my right hand, Helm Crag and Dunmail Raise on my left. Grasmere plain soon lay far below. The haymakers, encouraged by a gleam of sunshine, were hastily raking together the rain-blackened hay. From my outlook they appeared to be slowly and laboriously rolling up a great sheet of dark brown paper, uncovering beneath it one of the most fresh and vivid green. The mown grass is so long in curing in this country (frequently two weeks) that the new blades spring beneath it, and a second crop is well under way before the old is "carried." The long mountain slopes up which I was making my way were as verdant as the plain below me. Large coarse ferns or bracken, with an under-lining of fine grass, covered the ground on the lower portions. On the higher, grass alone prevailed. On the top of the divide, looking down into the valley of Ulleswater, I came upon one of those black tarns, or mountain lakelets, which are such a feature in this strange scenery. The word "tarn" has no meaning with us, though our young poets sometimes use it as they do this Yorkshire word "wold"; one they get from Wordsworth, the other from Tennyson. But when you have seen one of those still, inky pools at the head of a silent, lonely Westmoreland dale, you will not be apt to misapply the word in future. Suddenly the serene shepherd mountain opens this black, gleaming eye at your feet, and it is all the more weird for having no eyebrow of rocks, or fringe of rush or bush. The steep, encircling slopes drop down and hem it about with the most green and uniform turf. If its rim had been modeled by human hands, it could not have been more regular or gentle in outline. Beneath its emerald coat the soil is black and peaty, which accounts for the hue of the water and the dark line that encircles it.

> All round this pool both flocks and herds might drink
> On its firm margin, even as from a well,
> Or some stone-basin which the herdsman's hand
> Had shaped for their refreshment.

The path led across the outlet of the tarn, and then divided, one branch going down into the head of Grisedale, and the other mounting up the steep flank of Helvellyn. Far up the green acclivity I met a man and two young women making their way slowly down. They had come from Glenridding on Ulleswater, and were going to Grasmere. The women looked cold, and said I would find it wintry on the summit.

Helvellyn has a broad flank and a long back, and comes to a head very slowly and gently. You reach a wire fence well up on the top that divides some sheep ranges, pass through a gate, and have a mile yet to the highest ground in front of you; but you could traverse it in a buggy, it is so smooth and grassy. The grass fails just before the summit is reached, and the ground is covered with small fragments of the decomposed rock. The view is impressive, and such as one likes to sit down to and drink in slowly,— a

> Grand terraqueous spectacle,
> From centre to circumference, unveiled.

The wind was moderate and not cold. Toward Ulleswater the mountain drops down abruptly many hundred feet, but its vast western slope appeared one smooth, unbroken surface of grass. The following jottings in my note-book, on the spot, preserve some of the features of the scene: "All the northern landscape lies in the sunlight as far as Carlisle,

> A tumultuous waste of huge hill tops;

not quite so severe and rugged as the Scotch mountains, but the view more pleasing and more extensive than the one I got from Ben Venue. The black tarns at my feet, — Keppel Cove Tarn one of them, according to my map, — how curious they look! I can just discern the figure of a man moving by the marge of one of them. Away beyond Ulleswater is a vast sweep of country flecked here and there by slowly moving cloud shadows. To the northeast, in places, the backs and sides of the mountains have a green, pastoral voluptuousness, so smooth and full are they with thick turf. At other points the rock has fretted through the verdant carpet. St. Sunday's Crag to the west, across Grisedale, is a steep acclivity covered with small, loose stones, as if they had been dumped over the top, and were slowly sliding down; but nowhere do I see great boulders strewn about. Patches of black peat are here and there. The little rills, near and far, are white as milk, so swiftly do they run. On the more precipitous sides the grass and moss are lodged, and hold like snow, and are as tender in hue as the first April blades. A multitude of lakes are in view, and Morecambe Bay to the south. There are sheep everywhere, loosely scattered, with their lambs; occasionally I hear them bleat. No other sound is heard but the chirp of the mountain pipit. I see the wheat-ear flitting here and there. One mountain now lies in full sunshine, as fat as a seal, wrinkled and dimpled where it turns to the west, like a fat animal when it bends to lick itself. What a spectacle is now before me!—all the near mountains in shadow, and the distant in strong sunlight; I shall not see the like of that again. On some of the mountains the green vestments are in tatters and rags, so to speak, and barely cling to them. No heather in view. Toward Windermere the high peaks and crests are much more jagged and rocky. The air is filled with the same white, motionless vapor as in Scotland. When the sun breaks through,—

IN WORDSWORTH'S COUNTRY

Slant watery lights, from parting clouds, apace
Travel along the precipice's base,
Cheering its naked waste of scattered stone.

Amid these scenes one comes face to face with nature, with

the pristine earth,
The planet in its nakedness,

as he cannot in a wooded country. The primal, abysmal energies, grown tender and meditative, as it were, thoughtful of the shepherd and his flocks, and voiceful only in the leaping torrents, look out upon one near at hand and pass a mute recognition. Wordsworth perpetually refers to these hills and dales as lonely or lonesome; but his heart was still more lonely. The outward solitude was congenial to the isolation and profound privacy of his own soul. "Lonesome," he says of one of these mountain dales, but

Not melancholy — no, for it is green,
And bright, and fertile, furnished in itself
With the few needful things that life requires.
— In rugged arms how softly does it lie,
How tenderly protected!

It is this tender and sheltering character of the mountains of the Lake district that is one main source of their charm. So rugged and lofty, and yet so mellow and delicate! No shaggy, weedy growths or tangles anywhere; nothing wilder than the bracken, which at a distance looks as solid as the grass. The turf is as fine and thick

[269]

as that of a lawn. The dainty-nosed lambs could not crave a tenderer bite than it affords. The wool of the dams could hardly be softer to the foot. The last of July the grass was still short and thick, as if it never shot up a stalk and produced seed, but always remained a fine, close mat. Nothing was more unlike what I was used to at home than this universal tendency (the same is true in Scotland and in Wales) to grass, and, on the lower slopes, to bracken, as if these were the only two plants in nature. Many of these eminences in the north of England, too lofty for hills and too smooth for mountains, are called fells. The railway between Carlisle and Preston winds between them, as Houghill Fells, Tebay Fells, Shap Fells, etc. They are, even in midsummer, of such a vivid and uniform green that it seems as if they must have been painted. Nothing blurs or mars the hue; no stalk of weed or stem of dry grass. The scene, in singleness and purity of tint, rivals the blue of the sky. Nature does not seem to ripen and grow sere as autumn approaches, but wears the tints of May in October.

END OF VOLUME IX

The Riverside Press
CAMBRIDGE . MASSACHUSETTS
U . S . A